"The heels may be high, but I surely appreciate Rhonda Rhea's down-to-earth, genuine approach to Colossians 1:9–12. She offers a wise and witty description of what it means to walk worthy. *High Heels in High Places* will have you laughing one minute and then crying sweet tears of surrender to our loving God the next. This book, like its author, is unforgettable and totally captivating. It's one book you'll want to enjoy over and over."

Jennifer Rothschild, Women of Faith speaker;
author of *Lessons I Learned in the Dark*

"This book is witty, warm, whimsical, wise, and worthy of reading. Are you stepping in the footprints of Jesus? Rhonda walks us through these pages and shows us with stories and Scripture how we can walk in his steps and get closer and closer to him. Read and see—you'll be glad you did. The shoe might just fit!"

Thelma Wells, Women of Faith speaker;
president of A Woman of God Ministries;
author of *God Is Not Through with Me Yet*

"Rhonda Rhea has kicked up her heels in a creative, encouraging, hilarious manner that will have you laughing out loud while growing your faith. She skillfully weaves practical advice, personal anecdotes, and biblical wisdom into captivating chapters that speak truth to your soul while tickling your funny bone. Reading this book was like taking a walk with a very good friend who helped me enjoy the journey while leading me into a deeper relationship with God."

Carol Kent, speaker, author of *A New Kind of Normal*

high heels in high places

walking worthy in way cute shoes

Rhonda Rhea

Revell
Grand Rapids, Michigan

Published by Fleming H. Revell
a division of Baker Publishing Group
P.O. Box 6287, Grand Rapids, MI 49516-6287
www.revellbooks.com

Printed in the United States of America

Library of Congress Cataloging-in-Publication Data
Rhea, Rhonda.
   High heels in high places : walking worthy in way cute shoes / Rhonda Rhea.
      p.   cm.
   Includes bibliographical references.
   ISBN 10: 0-8007-3202-2 (pbk.)
   ISBN 978-0-8007-3202-8 (pbk.)
   1. Women—Religious life. I. Title.
BV4527.R48 2007
248.8′43—dc22   2007015307

To my prayer team,
the oh-so-special women who've invested extravagantly—
past, present, and future—
in inordinate, fervent, and focused prayer,
taking my life and ministry before the throne of God,
to the highest places in the most faithful way.

I'm blessed to follow in your high heel prints.

Janet Bridgeforth
Tina Byus
Diane Campbell
Mary Clark
Liz Clayton
Theresa Easterday
Shirley Farmer
Chris Hendrickson
Toni Hiles
Alberta Hutsler
Cindy Layman
Melinda Massey
Sheila McMichael
Peanuts Rudolph
Ann Trail

contents

acknowledgments

Thanks are always and ever due to my honey, Richie Rhea, my encourager and hero—Superhubby, Superpastor, Superman! What would I do without him? Richie's "more powerful than a locomotive" sermons and teachings and his "leaping tall buildings in a single bound" wisdom have been pointing me to "up, up, and away" kinds of higher places since our first meeting. Living with him and raising a family with him? It's everything wonderful. How blessed I am!

A "thanks" is almost too wimpy to offer the most dynamite kids a mom could have: Andrew (the most pleasant person and the most awesome songwriter I know), Jordan (megajokester, megamusician, and megamath whiz), Kaley (writer and friend after my own heart), Allie (my missionary-hearted sweetheart), and Daniel (the multimusically talented and way fun playmate of the group). My kids have so graciously supported, cheered, done a few extra dishes here and there, and offered all kinds of great material just by being their adorable and kooky selves. Did I mention how blessed I am?

Huge thanks to Pamela Harty of the Knight Agency, who is a special friend and such a wonderful agent. Does that make Pamela a "special agent"? I'll always be grateful she took me on as her own personal "Mission Impossible"—what an amazing writing industry missionary (or would that be "mission-*impossible*-ary"?).

I so appreciate Editor Extraordinaire, Jennifer Leep, and the wonderful publishing team at the Revell division of Baker Publishing Group. How glorious it is to have gifted, dedicated people working on this "heart of my heart" project.

Family-sized thanks to Troy First Baptist Church, for catching the vision for each project I turn out and running with it in the most supportive way. I'm so thankful for the encouragement of a church family who sees every part of my ministry as an extension of our church's ministry.

And special thanks to Halo & Wings, our local Christian book store here in Troy, Missouri, for encouraging, supplying, helping, and getting customers in headlocks in front of the Rhonda Rhea shelf (in the most loving way, I'm sure).

First and foremost and at every bottom line of every thanks I'll ever give, my biggest gratitude goes to my Lord and Savior, Jesus Christ—who constantly proves through my life that he truly can use *anyone*. How honored and blessed I am to be called his child and to be able to do what I do. I have the best job in the world. It's all because of him. And who else could carry me through every step of a high heels journey? All thanks, glory, praise, and honor to Jesus!

We are asking that you may be filled with the knowledge of His will in all wisdom and spiritual understanding, so that you may **walk worthy** of the Lord, fully pleasing to Him, bearing fruit in every good work and growing in the knowledge of God. May you be strengthened with all power, according to His glorious might, for all endurance and patience, with joy giving thanks to the Father, who has enabled you to share in the saints' inheritance in the light.

Colossians 1:9–12 HCSB

introduction

"We are asking . . ."

Okay, I confess. I'm a total shoe glutton. There's something wonderfully loyal about shoes. Outfits can turn on you. Your favorite dress, for instance, can hang innocently in the closet for months. Then when you want to wear it . . . bam! A size and a half too small! I pulled my little black dress out of the closet recently (you know, the one that's supposed to always remain faithful). It took one look at my thighs and doubled over in mocking laughter. Clothes can be so malicious.

But shoes? They never snicker. They could care less about your thighs. You can even pull them out right after the Christmas holidays, and you won't hear a peep out of them. Ya gotta love shoes.

Every time I clean out my closet, I realize how much I must love shoes. Pumps, tennies, loafers, boots, flats, heels—and those are just the ones in black. I won't even tell you how many I have in tan. I don't think I'll even tell you how many various shades of tan I've discovered. And I seem to find at least one pair in every hue. Exactly how many feet do I have? Oh well, I guess there's only one way to glut: big.

Shoeless in St. Louie

Would you believe that even though I have all those shoes—in style and out, with buttons, buckles, and bows, in every color and texture—still I can pull out the must-wear outfit for the evening and not have a single pair of shoes in the bunch that's right for the look! Some may think me a little shallow. I like to think of myself instead as a bit of a shoe overachiever. Of course, I also like to think of myself as a woman with thighs that are never mocked by a merciless black dress. Overachiever. Shallow gal. Fine line. I guess if I'm perfectly honest, I have to admit that I have at least a handful of shallow moments even in a good day. More if I'm trying on the black dress.

It's also really weird that, despite the overcrowding in the shoe section of my closet, every time I'm out shopping, I still seem to run into another pair just begging to come home with me. And if the shoe begs, buy it, right? Of course, after twenty-plus years of begging and buying, I need to do some major remodeling in my closet. I'm thinking of asking my husband for a closet more in tune with my space needs—say, a closet the size of *New Jersey*. Hey, if you're going to ask, why not ask big?

Asking High

Paul did some big asking. In Colossians 1:9–12 he asks for these biggies:

> We are asking that you may be filled with the knowledge of His will in all wisdom and spiritual understanding, so that you may walk

worthy of the Lord, fully pleasing to Him, bearing fruit in every good work and growing in the knowledge of God. May you be strengthened with all power, according to His glorious might, for all endurance and patience, with joy giving thanks to the Father, who has enabled you to share in the saints' inheritance in the light.

HCSB

Now there's some big asking! It's *high* asking. He's asking God to take the people he loves to higher places. And I think he's asking those people he loves to take some steps of faith. They're steps toward a deeper, richer relationship with a holy God.

For every woman in any and every kind of shoe, there are higher places to go in her walk with Christ. Yes, even we shallow girls can go higher and deeper. This book is designed to help us cultivate that longing to go there, and then give some how-tos straight from the Word of God. But no one said the journey to higher places had to be dull! Why not make the journey with a little fall-off-your-stilettos laughter along the way?

"We Are Asking"

Paul asked. Let's ask too. Let's ask to go higher places—to have a richer, more meaningful walk with Christ. Don't be uneasy if you've never dared to tread in high places before. We'll walk together. Whether you just need a little reminder or two to keep looking up and aspiring to go higher with him, or you're a little unfamiliar with the walk on the high side, the passage from Colossians 1 can be the perfect, most comfy fit for where you're going. We're encouraged in the passage to "walk worthy." That's the way to step into a higher, closer relationship with our heavenly Father. It's the way to be not just an overachiever but a higher achiever.

Heavenly Father, we are asking that you take us to richer, higher places with you through the High Heels journey. Challenge us to walk in new places—in whatever kind of shoes we're sporting. We ask that you would allow us to know you more fully, love you more deeply, serve you more genuinely, and follow you more closely. May we walk more worthy and may we honor you completely. All glory and praise to you!

Thank you for the gift of your Word. Thank you that when we really look at it and study it and make it a part of our lives, we're never, ever the same. Let us walk away from High Heels changed because of your loving work in our hearts as we look at the truths you've so graciously given us in your Word.

Thank you, Father, that you invented laughter. Thank you for calling us to a life of adventure and a life of great fun! I love to think of how you enjoy our pleasure. Thank you! I pray that you will fill our High Heels journey with laughter and joy—the kind that will make you smile too.

I pray for the one reading right now. If she needs encouragement, I pray she will be lifted up. If she needs discipline, I pray you'll grant it. If she needs joy, I ask that you please give it to her in big, falling-over doses—in the biggest, best way. If she has any need at all, I pray you will meet her exactly where she is and meet even her most personal needs. If one of those needs is a need to make a change, I pray she'll be confronted by your Word and in your most gracious love. Give her reminders of that extravagant, unconditional, glorious love you have for her every step of the way.

Oh Lord, take us to higher places with you!

part 1

"that you may be filled with the knowledge of his will"

it's all about the shoes

I was in a hurry to get ready—no surprise there. I'm a last-minute, use-that-panic-driven-rush-of-adrenaline kind of person. One of these days I'll deal with my tendency to procrastinate. For now I'm putting it off.

I was down to the last few readying details with negative-five minutes left. You should've seen me in major multitask mode. Multitasking is a very important skill for a procrastinator—and I must say, I was pretty impressive. In proctrastinator/multitasker mode, I was just about ready for takeoff. I was scooping up my purse and snatching the keys, putting on the last earring and slipping on my shoes—all while flying toward the door.

Flight Disaster

That's when I noticed something was terribly wrong. The feet were still moving, but the shoes hadn't made it all the way on. And let me add, scientifically speaking, I had picked up velocity equal to the negative-five-minutes adrenaline factor and fueled it with two strong cups of coffee. We're talking breakneck speed. The upper part of my body was moving at that adrenaline-induced, breakneck speed, but the feet were going nowhere. Momentum Mayday! We're going down!

Fortunately, there was a chair nearby. I steered my flying upper body toward the chair and somehow managed to hit it. Everything would've been fine if I had been able to throw out my arms to catch myself. But my hands were full of all the stuff I had so impressively multigathered. I was going down with no landing gear!

Crash Investigation

It was a disaster. I did a total hairdo dive smack into the chair. Worse than breakneck speed, it was hairdo-demolishing speed. Do you know what a bad hair landing can do to the timetable when you're already five minutes off your scheduled takeoff?

Before sorting out the hair damage, I looked down to find out what in the world had gone wrong with the shoes. The crash investigation revealed it was a mouse. No, not a live one. A live mouse in my shoe could've caused an entirely different kind of takeoff—and probably some major fuel leakage. It was the cat's catnip-filled mouse buddy.

Why Sammy thought my shoe was a good place to store his little friend is beyond me. All I know is that there was not only science at work, there was a mathematic equation I wasn't prepared for: one mouse-filled shoe + one hurrying foot = one big hair disaster.

Is It Really All About the Shoes?

When you're running late, here's a readying tip: try to remember to put *feet* in the shoes. Feet only. Nothing else. I finally made it to my destination that day, but I was plenty late and there was visible hair damage.

I've already confessed to being rather shoe-focused. Sometimes it's all about the shoes. But sometimes it isn't really about the shoes at all. Sometimes it's all about what you put in them.

It's like that when we want to go higher places with the Lord too. If we want to get to know the God of the universe in a richer and more personal way, we need to be "filled with the knowledge of his will." What's the first thing we need to do if we want to be filled with the knowledge of his will? We make sure we're not already filled with something else.

Before you can be filled, you might need to do some emptying. Are there worldly philosophies, sneaky lies, sinful habits, selfish thoughts you need to get rid of? Before you put on the shoes, get rid of the mouse.

We need to come to God completely empty of ourselves, ready to let him fill us up with himself. We need to get rid of sinfulness and self-centeredness—all those ego trips that result in our seeking our own agenda.

Take some time to get empty. Confess any sin and let him clean you up. Get rid of your own agenda and get revved up and ready to take off with his.

Fill 'Er Up!

Once we're empty, we're ready to be filled. Being filled with the knowledge of God's will begins with being filled with *him*. Ephesians 5:17 says to "understand what the Lord's will is." Then we're told what his will is in the next verse: "be filled with the Spirit."

Being filled with the Holy Spirit involves asking him to take control of every element of our lives moment by moment. It's letting his Spirit and the truth of his Word occupy and influence every part of our being—every thought, every word, every decision, every action—everything. When you ask him to do that, you're heading in a higher direction. You're flying straight toward being filled with the knowledge of his will!

Where's the School of God's Knowledge?

Ever wonder where you go to school for that kind of knowledge that takes you higher? You might be relieved to know that it's not about big titles or degrees. It's not about fancy words. It's not about being able to pray like the TV preachers. Our heavenly Father hasn't even ever asked that we be filled with the best multitasking skills. But can a person who's never trod in those theologically high places really be filled with the knowledge of his will? Oh yes!

My husband teaches a college philosophy class. He was away on a mission trip one week, and guess who had to fill in for him! Look out! Shallow gal heading to the deep end! Totally NOT my side of the pool. And the topic for the class I had to teach that day was—are you ready for this—Socrates. We're talking deep.

Deep Adventure

Fortunately, I'd seen *Bill and Ted's Excellent Adventure* so I was adequately and radically equipped. Teach on, dude!

Okay, I didn't use a lot of Bill and Ted's material. Actually, so much better than Bill and Ted, I have the testimony and the words of the apostle Paul in 1 Corinthians 2:1–5:

When I came to you, brothers, I did not come with eloquence or superior wisdom as I proclaimed to you the testimony about God.

For I resolved to know nothing while I was with you except Jesus Christ and him crucified. I came to you in weakness and fear, and with much trembling. My message and my preaching were not with wise and persuasive words, but with a demonstration of the Spirit's power, so that your faith might not rest on men's wisdom, but on God's power.

What is it that truly takes a woman who walks worthy into high places? What takes us to the deep side of the pool? Eloquence? Superior wisdom? Persuasive words? No, it's all about being filled up with Jesus! It's about having a testimony of the power of God at work in a life.

Instead of trying to pass myself off as a great philosopher in class that day (yeah, like they would've bought that anyway), I let them know what I really am. Weak. But praise God, I'm a walking testimony of the strength the Father gives to the weak. Being filled with the Spirit is being filled with power!

Hello, High Places!

It's so amazing that we can step into shallow places, then suddenly find ourselves taking flight into the heights instead. Not taking flight in a bad shoe way—or even in our own strength. But brought to high places in the truly most excellent adventure and held there in the most loving way by the very grace of God and by the limitless power of his Holy Spirit.

Because it's all in *his* power, he can take even this shallow gal to the deepest places and to the very highest places. Move over, Socrates. We're ready to get empty and be filled!

That I'm not putting off.

So be careful how you live, not as fools but as those who are wise. Make the most of every opportunity for doing good in these evil days. Don't act thoughtlessly, but try to understand what the Lord wants you to do. Don't be drunk with wine, because that will ruin your life. Instead, let the Holy Spirit fill and control you. Then you will sing psalms and hymns and spiritual songs among yourselves, making music to the Lord in your hearts. And you will always give thanks for everything to God the Father in the name of our Lord Jesus Christ.

Ephesians 5:15–20 NLT

2

foot-notes

I don't know if there's anyone who can scope out a clearance rack quite like I can. It's almost embarrassing. Is there such a thing as shoe-sale radar? At least I don't usually beep when I'm tracking.

I was at the mall recently—not even shopping for shoes, incidentally—when across the department store I spotted a towering shoe rack. It was a thing of beauty. I think that's how archaeologists must feel when they make an amazing find. The tower could only mean one thing: Clearance! I was momentarily distracted by some annoying beeping, then realized it was me.

I shrugged off the beeps and targeted the sale rack. Fortunately there weren't any of those bothersome browsing kind of shoppers in my way. I would've hated to have to mow them over. That always seems tacky—especially when the shoppers are pushing strollers. No browsers or strollers. I had a clear path and I was on my way.

When I got to the clearance tower, however, I was hindered by several shoppers hovering in front of the size 5s. *Why did all these small-footed women have to shop today?* They had a defensive block with double coverage all the way from from the 5s to about half past the 6½s.

Have you ever seen one of those movies where the football hero dives over the top of the opposing team's defensive line to score an emotional and exceptionally rewarding touchdown? Okay, I didn't do it. But I thought about it. Being five foot tall, I decided to milk my shortness and try to blitz my way in from the bottom. I was still about four ladies and goal to go when I was stopped short (so to speak) by a secondary line of small women. Blindsided! How many five-foot women could there be at the mall at one time? What are the odds? I couldn't even punt.

When I finally elbowed and "excuse me'd" my way in, I realized it was worth the bruises. An entire row of shoes four or five stickers deep in markdowns. Touchdown! With a bonus price-sticker pileup! I love it when there's an orange sticker on top of a blue sticker on top of a green sticker on top of a white one. Rainbow markdowns!

Finding multicolored markdowns is sort of a sign, in my book. The sign reads BUY ME! It was like I was getting personal mail from at least one pair of those cute sale shoes. Could mail from a pair of shoes be called a foot-note?

I rarely ignore foot-notes. I don't ignore them, because I love bargain shoes. I love them so much that I'm willing to seek them out. I've done everything this side of tackling for the right shoes— and just barely this side, at that.

Let's Tackle This

Being filled with the knowledge of his will is all about seeking him so much more diligently than the cutest sale shoes. Truly seeking him. As you're seeking him, you become even more aware of this wonderful truth: *he wants you.* He wants every part of you every minute of every day.

So exactly how should we go about seeking him? The testimonies of some people might lead you to believe that seeking him is about a big emotional experience. But it's not. It's about asking God to do whatever he wants. We're seeking the knowledge of *his* will, not ours.

In the last chapter we talked about how we need to be empty of self and filled with his Spirit. We seek him by chasing down that filling with all our passion. It's coming to the place where we say to God, "I can't live without your filling. There is absolutely no way I can walk worthy without being filled up with you." If we want to walk worthy and please him, we have to seek his filling with all our hearts.

Halfhearted Seeking?

How many times have I become complacent? I don't even want to admit it. It's all too easy to settle. Why go higher places in the walk with Christ when life is really not all that bad here in the low life? I have my salvation. Eternity is settled. Shouldn't I be content with that?

But there is so much more. It's one thing to experience salvation. It's another to experience the *joy* of my salvation. Isaiah 12:3 says, "With joy you will draw water from the wells of salvation." It's better than a Gatorade shower at the end of a game! Joy in salvation is a result of fellowship with him. It's a result of being so filled with him that it bubbles right over and out of my life in the form of joy. Not sports drink bubbles—joy bubbles! Why should we be content with merely having salvation when we can live it to the bubbly fullest?

Being filled with the Spirit is a command. It's God's will. He promises to answer every prayer in his will. Ask and it will happen.

Don't think you have to clean up your life first. Confess your sin, yes, but let God do the cleanup. That's what he does best. When Paul wrote to the Ephesians to "be filled with the Spirit," there was still a lot of sinning going on. These people were saved out of some big-time depravity. But God is the one who does the saving. He's the one who does the filling. It's exactly what he wants for you, the child he adores.

Being filled with him is more than just getting rid of sin, though that's a big part of it. But it's also getting rid of self. Author and speaker Jennifer Rothschild wrote in her newsletter about a conference where she was slated to follow Beth Moore. Beth Moore! Talk about a tough act to follow!

Jennifer said she found herself fretting about it, full of Jennifer instead of full of God's Holy Spirit. But then she wrote about coming to the end of herself. She said, "I am desperate for God. If he doesn't fill me, I will fill myself, and the result is ugly. I need the whole of God to fill the whole of me."

Take a look at your life. Do you see joy that bubbles out as a result of being filled with the Holy Spirit of God? If not, stop and ask for it right now. It may mean you'll need to pray something like this: "Lord, I want to be filled with your Holy Spirit and bubbling over with your joy. Whatever it may cost me, I'm willing to pay it. Whatever you may ask me to give up, I will. I surrender all of me. Please fill me up with you."

Pray it and he will answer!

Higher Places for a Short Girl

Jennifer Rothschild later wrote, "Holiness is neither complicated nor self-propelled. It's not the sum of the thou-shalts and thou-shalt-nots. It's not merely the absence of sin, my friend; it's the absence of self. Holiness, simply put, is the whole of God filling the whole of me."[1]

That's my daily prayer when I'm rightly seeking to go higher places with him: *Fill the whole of me with the whole of you.*

Higher places for this short girl—who would've thought it possible? And for the record, any time I'm moving toward higher places with him, shoe shoppers blocking the 5s through the 6½s are so much safer.

> For we know, brothers loved by God, that he has chosen you, because our gospel came to you not simply with words, but also with power, with the Holy Spirit and with deep conviction. You know how we lived among you for your sake. You became imitators of us and of the Lord; in spite of severe suffering, you welcomed the message with the joy given by the Holy Spirit.
>
> *1 Thessalonians 1:4–6*

---

3   what's your shoe size?

Why do we women tend to want to be at least one shoe size smaller than we really are? I'm not sure any of us really know why, but the shoe-shopping adage seems to go: "If the shoe fits, try a size smaller." What is it we love about tiny feet? Is it some kind of subconscious leftover Barbie influence from our doll days?

If you think your Mattel-induced delusions might be buried somewhere in a Barbie-shaped corner of your subconscious, here are some cues you're under the influence.

Top Ten Ways You Can Tell You're Having Barbie Flashbacks

10. You think your waist should be the same size as your wrist.
 9. You try to get your hair to curl in one giant blond wave that swoops out about three feet past your shoulders.
 8. You never blink.
 7. You ignore all laws of physics and toss out the reality that if anyone actually tried to give you a Barbie-sized bosom above your wrist-sized waist, your spine would snap like a dry twig.
 6. You're tempted to wear your stilettos with your swimsuit.
 5. You try to find other places to store those things that seem to be getting in the way of your perfect shape—like your liver, spleen, kidneys, vertebrae . . . Who needs 'em?
 4. You forget you really can look down.
 3. You go shopping for a pink plastic convertible.
 2. Your mother has never had a reason to nag you about your posture.
 1. Your cell phone has a speed dial for Dr. 90210.

Sizing It Up

Isn't it likely that the desire for Barbie feet spurned the invention of high heels in the first place? They're just so cute! But if we want those lash-length feet, the Barbie way is to disproportionately (in keeping with all her other disproportions) keep nine-tenths of the foot in a vertical position. A foot that folds a couple of times at ninety-degree angles looks four sizes smaller than it really is. The foot is prone to snap, of course, but it will definitely look smaller.

Has anyone else ever noticed that after a long day in those heels, Barbie would slide those rascals off, but her feet would still be frozen in the shape of a lightning bolt? Poor thing. I'm not sure if I'm willing to have petrified accordion feet to be cute. What's the use in having Ken and a Dream House if you're in too much pain to enjoy them?

The long and short of it is, if you want to actually *walk* in the shoes, they need to be at least somewhere close to your size. And if you really want to know the right size, it's a good idea to measure.

When we're sizing up a life decision, how do we measure what's right and what's wrong? When it's time to take a step, how do we calculate the wisest choices? There's only one true measuring stick when it comes to truth: God's Word.

What is your next step in studying God's Word? Maybe you've never picked it up and read it for yourself. Maybe you've been giving it a casual read and it's time to go higher places in deeper study. Maybe you're seeking God's next step toward higher places for you in studying his Word.

Seeking Him through His Word

Studying the Bible is expressly connected to the last chapter's topic of desperately seeking him with everything we are. But did you know that even before you seek him, he's already been seeking you? Yes, he is seeking you!

Jesus told three incredible stories in Luke 15. He tells a story of a shepherd who left ninety-nine sheep to find the lost one. Then the shepherd carried the lamb home and gathered his friends and neighbors for a big rejoicing party. He tells the story of a woman who lost a coin and then wraps up with the story of the lost son and his seeking father.

Lost sheep. Lost coin. Lost son. In all three stories, the lost was sought. In all three instances there was a giant party when the lost was found. Seek, seek, seek, then party, party, party. I love the part of the story of the lost son when the father comes running to his son, hugs him, kisses him, and—you guessed it—throws a party. I love it because I can picture the Father running to me. Imagine! And you can picture the Father running to you. He seeks you. He desires to be with you. What an amazing truth! When we pick up his Word, it's like our way of running back to him for the sweetest party.

Every time you study God's Word, there's an embrace. He's running to you with his message. You can run back by listening to what he has to say to you as you read, study, meditate on, and memorize his Word.

And the Bible really is our one true measuring tool. It shows us truth, it shows us ways the Father is seeking us, and it shows us where to walk. God's Word is like a GPS for our feet. Psalm 25:4–5 says, "Show me the path where I should walk, O LORD; point out the right road for me to follow. Lead me by your truth and teach me, for you are the God who saves me. All day long I put my hope in you" (NLT).

Wouldn't it be nice if, along with the GPS, the Lord made knowing his will in every decision as clear as a giant sale banner on the front of your favorite shoe store? Should I buy those shoes? Take that job? Purchase that house? Marry that guy? No doubt there have been times all of us have wanted a billboard or skywriting kind of answer from God. Sometimes he makes it just about that clear. But part of being filled with the knowledge of his will is developing the discipline of seeking it. Seeking to know his will is about knowing HIM. He is so gracious to have given us his Word so we can know him. And as we know him more and more, we find those higher places in communion with him.

Sky Writing vs. High Writing

As we grow closer to him, treading in those higher places, he directs our thinking. He directs our paths. Proverbs 3:5–6 says,

> Lean on, trust in, and be confident in the Lord with all your heart and mind and do not rely on your own insight or understanding. In all your ways know, recognize, and acknowledge Him, and He will direct and make straight and plain your paths.
>
> AMP

When we lean on and trust him to direct our understanding, he can actually transform our thinking so that we can truly know what he wants us to do—without the billboards or skywriting. We don't need skywriting. We need his "higher than the sky" writing to take us to those higher places!

God doesn't want us to search for his will because he wants to make it something secret and illusive. He wants us to know his will clearly. But he wants us to seek his will because he wants us to seek *him*. To come to him in prayer, to pore over his Word, to truly seek him.

All Barbie moments aside, we find every measure of truth and we are filled with the joyful knowledge of his will by seeking, studying, and taking to heart his law. "I take joy in doing your will, my God, for your law is written on my heart" (Ps. 40:8, NLT). We're filled with the knowledge of his will as we let his Word shape us—and there is such joy there! Party, party, party!

There's also joy in knowing you really don't have to be Barbie-shaped or wear Barbie-type six-inch stilettos to go higher places. As a matter of fact, it's good to know that when you give up on the Barbie look, you actually get to keep your liver and kidneys.

> Give me understanding and I will obey your law; I will put it into practice with all my heart. Make me walk along the path of your commands, for that is where my happiness is found.
>
> *Psalm 119:34–35 NLT*

wake up, step up, pray up 4

Off with the heels, on with the tennies. I wish I could say I find great joy in pushing aside my cutest high heels and tying on my workout shoes. I also wish I didn't have to admit to a bad aerobic attitude; I roll my eyes every time I tie on my tennies. If eye rolls were aerobic, I would be one fit chick. I could just take the tennies right back off, curl up in my warm bed, and snooze for another forty minutes.

No sleep after a wake-up call, though. The wake-up call came the day before starting the new exercise program. I was trying to squeeze into my new skirt (not too distantly related to that rebelliously mocking little black dress). There was more hip action trying to writhe into the skirt than I would even have dared put into an exercise routine. Aerobic? Maybe. Pretty? I can't begin to tell you how NOT pretty it was. Not pretty getting the skirt on. Not pretty once it was on.

I use the term "on" loosely, because when I finally managed to squirm into the skirt, I realized if I wanted to zip the thing, I could only keep one of my buns. Who attached all the extra chub to my backside? That's when I heard the alarm. Definite wake-up call. Unless I was going in for at least a partial bun-ectomy, I would have to be make lifestyle changes. *Argh.* Exercise.

So there it was, the first day of yet another new exercise routine. One more of those "first day of the rest of your life" things—only not necessarily the pleasant kind. I thought about trying an outdoor regimen until I remembered that not only does nature cause me to do a "too hot" or "too cold" or "too many bugs" whine, but putting on those last ten bun-pounds had added a lot more wind resistance than I had before. I think I had enough poundage to keep me from taking flight, but still, who needs to be mocked by the wind?

On a Roll (Eyes Only)

I settled on an indoor routine and rolled my eyes for at least the tenth time. Tennis shoes tied and eyes sufficiently rolled, I was ready to call it a morning and grab a mug of latte and a sticky bun. Did I say "bun"? Another eye roll. I prayed for a better attitude through the first fifteen minutes of exercise. The last fifteen minutes I prayed something more like, "Lord Jesus, come quickly."

Probably not one of my more spiritually mature prayer moments.

Every day should be a wake-up reminder that prayer is an enormously high privilege. If we truly want to be filled with the knowledge of his will, then we need to stay faithful in prayer.

Do we even really comprehend what power there is in prayer? Are our minds and hearts adequately wired to take in the earth-shaking might? In the simplest terms, there are no higher places for us if we're neglecting this source of power. When you think about it, is there any higher place than the intimacy we find with God as we're seeking him in prayer? This is where we'll find the sweetest fellowship with our unseen holy God.

There's such power in the intimacy of prayer. Not the power found in our words, but the power found in him. If your prayer life is weak, then there's no doubt your next step to higher places needs to be not so much stepping as kneeling. Prayer is crucial to going higher and getting closer to the Father. Wellington Boone said it so well in his book *Breaking Through*:

> God is calling us into the closet of intimacy with Him. In this set-apart time, God breaks through to our hearts. From this distinct and mandatory place of growth in Him, we not only experience our breakthrough, but we become available to seed breakthrough in other people's hearts. We become the fruit of the intentions of the Lord. As we surrender to Him, we become the offering that God gives on earth to a dying world. Do you claim devotion to God and rarely darken the door of your prayer closet? God is calling you to greater intimacy. He wants to take you to the deep waters of fellowship with Himself.[2]

The Prayer Necessities

If you want to go higher places, special times of prayer are vital to a healthy connection to the Lord. Reading his Word and praying to him are two things that build those oh-so-important closer and higher bonds with the Father. We need to be faithfully committed. Romans 12:12 says, "Be joyful in hope, patient in affliction, faithful in prayer." The more faithful we are in prayer, the more power we have to stay joyful and to show patience. Here are a few things to remember as you think about prayer power and your quiet time with the Lord.

Find the Right Time and the Right Place. Set a time that will work best for you. Sometimes schedules get crazy and we have to be flexible. And that's okay. But keep in mind that consistency can help build good habits of faithfulness into your special prayer times. The time and place you choose for your prayer time should be as distraction-free as possible. It may need to be during the kids' nap time or early in the morning before the kids are up or before you get ready for work. And you may need to shove any petty distractions (like that way-tight skirt) out of sight, out of mind, during this time.

Praise Him, Thank Him, and Pray through His Word. Your prayer time should include praying through Bible passages, praising the Lord for who he is, and thanking him for what he's done. We need to be careful that our prayer time doesn't become a big to-do list that we hand the Father. It should be about him, not us. When we're praying through Scripture, we know we're praying in his will.

Confess Sin, Ask for and Accept His Forgiveness. As we think about who he is and his amazing holiness, our unholiness becomes all too clear. Ask the Lord to reveal to you any sin you need to confess. Give your sin a good dose of 1 John 1:9: "But if we confess our sins to him, he is faithful and just to forgive us and to cleanse us from every wrong" (NLT). Confess your sin and accept his gracious forgiveness (and you can look again at confessing sin in chapter 7).

Ask Him to Meet the Needs of Others. "Me-centered" prayer is not a higher places kind of prayer. Paul gives us some pretty ambitious prayer direction in 1 Timothy 2:1 when he tells us to pray for everyone. "I urge you, first of all, to pray for all people. As you make your requests, plead for God's mercy upon them" (NLT). Pray for all people? There's a challenge! Let Paul's challenge remind you to take the needs of your family, your friends, your church, and your government to the Lord in prayer. Your heavenly Father will meet you there.

The Highest Praying

Prayer is such a high gift. And it's such a high gift when someone prays for us. Peter experienced one of the highest of high prayer moments when Jesus told him that he, the Lord of Lords, King of Kings, had prayed for him. In Luke 22:32, shortly before Jesus's crucifixion, we read the words Jesus said right to Peter's face, "I have prayed for you." Is there any higher prayer?

Guess what? Those highest of high prayer moments are yours too. Jesus has prayed for you! John 17:6–19 is Jesus's amazing, gracious prayer for all who are his. If you've given your life to Christ, you're included in the glorious "them" in verse 9 when Jesus said, "I pray for them." Imagine, the one who holds the universe together praying for you!

Jesus knows how to pray so much more completely than we do. A few verses later in the passage in Luke, Jesus prayed in Gethsemane. He asked his disciples to pray too. What a contrast in the way Jesus prayed and the way his disciples prayed. Jesus sought the Father with intense fervor, so earnestly that he was sweating blood. The disciples? They dozed off.

I wonder if there's a connection between the disciples snoozing and their state of mind just a few verses before when they were arguing about which one of them would go down in history as the greatest. Pretty prideful, selfish stuff. But when Jesus prayed in Gethsemane, he prayed for his Father's will—even though he knew that meant his own horrendous suffering. They were prayers of surrender, prayers of complete humility and definitive selflessness.

No-Dozers

Our goal in our prayer lives should always be to come surrendered, humble, selfless—and to pray fervently. Not dozing off, but striving to become powerful no-dozers in our prayer lives. When Jesus finished his ardent prayer and then found his disciples sleeping, he said to them, "Why are you asleep? Wake up and pray that you won't be tested" (Luke 22:46 CEV). We open ourselves up to temptation and testing when we don't stay fervent in prayer. Succumbing to temptation leads to lower, not higher, places.

Let's allow this be our wake-up call to prayer. Alarm buzzing. Going higher places with the Father in prayer means we need to be willing to pray like Jesus—humbly, selflessly, and fervently—just as going to slimmer places in skinny skirts may mean we need to be willing to tie on the tennies and do some major sweating. Painful? Yes. But in the long run, I figure it still has to be less painful for this poor body than a partial bun-ectomy.

Speaking of my body, if I decided to vote on which part of me should win the "Fittest Body Part" award, it would be no contest. It's the part of me that does the most rolling. The eyes have it!

Exercise daily in God—no spiritual flabbiness, please! Workouts in the gymnasium are useful, but a disciplined life in God is far more so, making you fit both today and forever. You can count on this. Take it to heart. This is why we've thrown ourselves into this venture so totally. We're banking on the living God, Savior of all men and women, especially believers.

1 Timothy 4:7–10 Message

part 2

"in all wisdom and
spiritual understanding"

baby steps are for . . . well . . . babies   5

Don't you just love a new pair of white heels? I'm almost sure a spanking new pair of white shoes puts a little extra sass in a walk. You have to love strutting your stuff in the cutest new shoes of a new season. Unless, that is, it's a little too early in the season.

My first "new white shoes" experience of the season a few years ago happened in the wet beginning of a muddy spring. Could there be anything more disturbing than stepping out of the car and sinking ankle deep into a muck puddle? Picture me stuck in the muck—needing a tow truck. Poetic, but not pretty.

I was gloomier than the wet weather when I pulled my foot out of that puddle and heard that sucking *th-th-thwup* sound. The shoe? Sadly, it was no longer white. It was no longer discernible as a shoe, for that matter. What time of the year is a furry-looking, twig-covered, mud-brown ankle boot in style?

Heel Issues

As a kid, I remember being pretty confused about one of the big shoe questions of life: When is it really okay to wear white shoes?

Does the "no white after Labor Day" law apply to purses too? Where does white trim fit in? What about light beige? And what do we do now that there's a color called "winter white"? Big issues.

Okay, I'm kidding. I know shoe color is not exactly the biggest life or death issue of the year. Spring happens whether I'm dressed for it or not, just as the flowers bloom with or without pastel accessories. But I have to tell you, it's a pretty good feeling when I know without a doubt I'm wearing an outfit that matches up with the season. I admit I would be some kind of uncomfortable if I really did have to wear furry brown ankle boots to a Labor Day gathering. Muddy snow boots in the summer? I would be uncomfortable even if I had a matching woolly trimmed scarf. Uncomfortable and bizarre-looking. The look would be bizarre even minus the mud—and I would rather have my bizarre looks stand on their own without considering the season, thank you very much.

Talk about Bizarre

It's even more uncomfortable when we say we know God in the most intimate way, yet don't do what he says. It's exactly the opposite of heading to those higher places with him. First John 2:3–6 says,

> Here's how we can be sure that we know God in the right way: Keep his commandments. If someone claims, "I know him well!" but doesn't keep his commandments, he's obviously a liar. His life doesn't match his words. But the one who keeps God's word is the person in whom we see God's mature love. This is the only way to be sure we're in God. Anyone who claims to be intimate with God ought to live the same kind of life Jesus lived.
>
> Message

If I ever do make the bizarre decision to wear woolly boots on Labor Day, it's not likely to bring on a premature winter. Shoes don't really make the season. And obedience doesn't make a follower of God. But a follower of God will no doubt obey, or she's not truly a follower. Genuinely knowing him changes the way we live. Verse 29 in that same chapter in 1 John says, "Once you're convinced that he is right and righteous, you'll recognize that all who practice righteousness are God's true children" (Message).

Our obedience can take us to higher places with Christ. Our lack of obedience can leave us stuck in the muck trying to do something fruitful but ending up with a bunch of mud pies instead. That's such baby stuff. It's time to grow up. Obedience is a higher-places kind of evidence that we know him and love him. In John 14:15, Jesus said it plainly: "If you love me, you will obey what I command."

I think Jesus loves to tell us these kinds of things plainly. When he called his disciples, he simply said, "Come, follow me." Can you picture looking into the eyes of the one who created the entire universe? Can you imagine having the idea soak into your thinking that he would even desire to have you follow him? What an honor! At that point of his calling to follow—our utmost honor—can you even remotely imagine looking into those eyes and saying, "No, I don't think so"? Unthinkable!

Shiny Designer Shoes

Following him has such an astounding impact on life. It's what we were designed to do. If you'd like to see your life path light up ever so much more brilliantly than even the shiniest new white shoes, follow him. The old hymn says it so well:

Footprints of Jesus that make the pathway glow;
We will follow the steps of Jesus, where e'er they go.[3]

Growing up in obedience is forgetting about those baby steps. They really are for babies. There's maturity in learning to let our obedience match up with our heart's condition and in following him on that glowing path.

Wisdom and spiritual understanding happen when we obey. Look again at Psalm 119:33–35: "Teach me, O LORD, to follow every one of your principles. Give me understanding and I will obey your law: I will put it into practice with all my heart. *Make me walk along the path of your commands, for that is where my happiness is found*" (NLT, emphasis mine). Exactly where our high heels should be trodding: along the path of his commands. And don't you just love what this verse tells us we find all along the path? Happiness!

How about that! We get the blessing of finding real wisdom and spiritual understanding, only to discover it comes with the delightful accessory of happiness. It's happiness that doesn't fade when things are not going perfectly—when we're ankle deep in one of life's puddles. It doesn't fade in and out with the season. It's always there. In spring, summer, fall, or winter white.

Jesus replied, "If anyone loves me, he will obey my teaching. My Father will love him, and we will come to him and make our home with him. He who does not love me will not obey my teaching. These words you hear are not my own; they belong to the Father who sent me.

"All this I have spoken while still with you. But the Counselor, the Holy Spirit, whom the Father will send in my name, will teach you all things and will remind you of everything I have said to you. Peace I leave with you; my peace I give you. I do not give to you as the world gives. Do not let your hearts be troubled and do not be afraid."

John 14:23–27

the shoe's on the other foot   6

You can usually depend on good fashion counsel from your best girlfriends. You have to have a girlfriend nearby to tell you if you're wearing the right shoes with your outfit. And a girlfriend is, of course, vital for a back-of-the-hair check. The last thing any of us want is to head off to an important event with a back-of-the-head hair hole. The worst!

The department store ladies are good in a pinch to help you make the right shoe call, though I think sometimes their counsel has more to do with which shoe brings the biggest commission instead of which one looks best with your outfit. But husbands? I don't mean to be tacky, but have you ever put a different shoe on each foot and asked your husband which one looks best with your outfit? I've noticed when I ask my hubby for shoe advice, his face suddenly gets that distressed look. When I look in the mirror and see that same kind of distressed look on my own face, I know I need a day at the spa and some serious chocolate. In basic male paraphrase, a day at the spa equals eighteen holes of golf, and serious chocolate is usually equivalent to large portions of undercooked red meat.

If you put a different shoe on each foot and you're having trouble deciding which one to wear, before you ask your husband for a shoe consult, you may want to watch out for certain clues that he might not give you the best answer.

The Top Ten Signs Your Husband Might Not Be the Best One to Help You with Your Shoe Decision

10. You hear him whispering under his breath, "Eenie, meenie, minie . . ."
9. He pulls out his tire gauge and asks if the right one needs a little air.
8. He picks the one that most reminds him of his favorite meal (if a shoe reminds him of fried chicken, that can't be good, can it?).
7. He asks which shoe is the most comfortable (Puh-lease—like we would ever remotely consider that factor in determining which shoe to wear).
6. He tries to caulk one of them.
5. You ask him when he's in his recliner, and he answers between snores but never completely opens his eyes (shoe decisions made during REM are rarely dependable).
4. He says he likes the left one because it reminds him of the color of his belt sander.
3. He won't answer until he tries them on himself (that's when you need to hide all your shoes and get him a good counselor).
2. He asks which one has the least miles on it.
1. He doesn't notice that the two shoes are different.

Guys tend to have Sunday shoes, casual shoes, and tennis shoes. Maybe golf shoes if they're fairly shoe extravagant. Four pairs of shoes? Who could live like that? Gotta have shoes!

I depend on a large shoe selection almost as much as I depend on the gal who does my hair. Okay, that may be an exaggeration, but we're talking major dependence here.

A Rich Hair-itage

I do *so* depend on the gal who does my hair (that's not just "hair-say"). I come from a long line of follicly dependent people. There's a certain trust between a woman and her hairdresser. Every time I go in, I put my hair in her hands (incidentally, in return, she puts her hands in my hair).

I knew it was time to go in last week. Having grayed early in life, I have to be careful not to get that parfait look. White layer, chocolate layer looks good in a dessert but not necessarily on a head. It's a lot like the chicken/shoe thing. When I glanced in the mirror and noticed a white skunk stripe down the center, I knew it was past time. The Cruella De Vil look is just not me.

It's even worse when I'm not the only one who notices. I hate it when a tall person looks down at the top of my head (being five foot zero has definite hair disadvantages) and says in a bull-horn voice, "Do not look directly into the roots—corneal damage may occur!" It's one thing for people to be blinded by my beauty (*ahem*), but this is something entirely different.

So I went in a few days ago for my hair fix. I freely confess my chemical dependence on hair products, and I don't want an intervention, thanks anyway. It was practically magic. In just an hour or so, voilà! I was transformed! No corneal damage, no *Touched by an Angel* kind of scalp-glow happening—just good hair. Did I mention I love my hair gal? What would I do without her?

While I'm confessing my dependence, let me just say that I have another dependency issue that's eternally more significant. I'm depending on my heavenly Father for so much more than good shoes and hair. He is my very life. Isaiah 26:3–5 says, "People with their minds set on you, you keep completely whole, steady on their feet, because they keep at it and don't quit. Depend on God and keep at it because in the Lord God you have a sure thing" (Message). We're likely good and convinced that growing up in obedience is important. We need to be just as sure that one of the most practical ways we grow up in obedience is to grow up in dependence.

Dependence Is In

The "in" colors are sure to come and go—in hair, shoes, and other related necessities. But our God is a sure thing—ever steady, ever dependable. He's our one true necessity. And I can trust him with all of me, from the very root of every hair right down to the pointy tips of my shoes (even if the shoes don't match each other). Relying on him for everything I need in life provides a rest, a peace, and an unexplainable joy that doesn't have anything to do with circumstances. He gives peace and joy even on bad-hair days. It's better than magic! Dependence on the Lord has a powerful way of transforming a life. And it never goes out of style.

"Growing up" and "growing dependent" may sound like opposites. But understanding this deep spiritual truth can be the very thing that takes you to your next level—to a higher place with your Lord: maturing is depending more fully on him.

We have to depend on our heavenly Father for every step. Every breath.

As a matter of fact, our dependence on him should be much like breathing. How often do we take a breath and then think to ourselves, "That'll hold me for a while. Maybe I'll suck in some more air next week or so"? Depending on him and drawing from him through prayer and through his Word are like manna. When God fed the children of Israel as they were wandering in the wilderness, any time they tried to stuff away an extra portion of the manna he provided for the day, it would turn disgusting and wormy. His mercies are new every morning. Lamentations 3:23–24 reminds us, "The LORD can always be trusted to show mercy each morning. Deep in my heart I say, 'The LORD is all I need; I can depend on him!'" (CEV).

Mercy Me

You need a new and fresh dose of God's grace and mercy for every new day. Yesterday's fellowship may have been sweet, but if you try to stretch it into the next day, you get a moldy mess. Let him give you a fresh new touch of grace for every day. Depend on him for that touch. That is his desire—and it's your great blessing. Ignore this one thing, and you won't reach those higher places. You'll stay in the shallow walk, looking up, wishing to get to that high and close walk with your Father, but frustrated that it's always out of reach. You'll find spiritual understanding as you depend on him day by day.

It requires discipline. Some days you may have to be still. Psalm 131:1–2 says, "Lord, my heart is not proud; my eyes are not haughty. I don't concern myself with matters too great or awesome for me. But I have stilled and quieted myself, just as a small child is quiet with its mother. Yes, like a small child is my soul within me" (NLT). Quiet yourself before God and let him know that you will wait there until you know, truly know, that he is near. Worship him, spend time with him, depend on him for your every need. He knows you inside out, and you can trust him. He has even numbered the hairs on your head.

Hmm, I wonder if he has the hairs sorted by number and by color too. Mine would be hard to peg.

> We depend on the LORD alone to save us.
>> Only he can help us, protecting us like a shield.
> In him our hearts rejoice,
>> for we are trusting in his holy name.
> Let your unfailing love surround us, LORD,
>> For our hope is in you alone.
>
> *Psalm 33:20–22 NLT*

7

heels on wheels

I'm so glad the cutest shoes rarely roll. I've seen kids with those roller tennies. Rolling children scare me just a little.

Since we already have roller-shoe technology, it's certainly feasible that one of these days it could come into vogue in the high heels zone. I can picture models gliding down the runway at impressive velocities. Fashion designers could squeeze three or four times the number of outfits into a fashion show. The outfits would likely be a big blur, but lots of outfits, nonetheless.

You probably know by now that I have enough trouble staying upright even without the wheels. Chapter 1's nosedive/hair disaster is a good case in point. Can you picture a scene like that on rollers?

Roll 'Em

While none of my high heels roll, I spend so much time carting teens and their friends back and forth in my minivan—wheels spinning wildly and constantly underneath me—that it sometimes seems like these van wheels are an extension of my outfit anyway.

Of course, I also call my minivan a milk-mobile. With a houseful of teens, it would frighten you to know how much milk I have to buy in a week. Let's just say sometimes it takes two or three of us to push the cart. When you buy so many gallons at a time, one of them is bound to get missed somewhere along the way. That "somewhere along the way" happened at exactly the wrong time of the year.

A few months ago, we had loaded about eight gallons of milk into the car, but never noticed that only seven made it into the house. That lost gallon was in the floor of the minivan under the last seat, lurking . . . plotting unspeakable evil.

Crying over Exploded Milk

It was during the dog days of summer and, of all times for the minivan to need a repair or two, that happened to be the week we had to put it in the shop. Three days in the shop. Three days of temperatures over a hundred degrees. The milk swelled up and—horror of horrors—exploded all over the car! Oh, the humanity. It lobbed milk shrapnel over the entire backseat. Milk? No, it was closer to CHEESE. And the smell! It was something like a barf-and-old-socks combo—with cabbage and liverwurst. The stench made it into every single nook and cranny of the vehicle. As bad as the milk/cheese cleanup was, nothing compared to the fallout we had to deal with for weeks. My eyes are watering just thinking about the stench. Oh well, no use crying over spilled cheese.

The great cottage cheese disaster was a good excuse to practice that certain cool driving look. All the windows are down, the left elbow edges just outside the driver-side window; the right hand hangs casually over the steering wheel. Of course, it's not nearly as cool when you're in a MINIVAN. But we still had plenty of chances to get the cool look down. We're talking about a lot of time riding with the windows down.

Taking care of sin issues in our lives is even more important than getting every gallon of milk out of a hot van. When left to simmer, those sin issues can explode all kinds of ugliness into our lives, and it can spill right over into the lives of those around us.

If you're sensing a swell of sin in your life, it's time to change direction—before there's a giant sin detonation of the stinkiest kind. As a matter of fact, the wisdom and spiritual understanding we're asking for happens as we change direction in just this way.

Changing Direction

The change of direction results from grasping that, before we can step into a higher life, we have to come to a realization that we're not high. As a matter of fact, we have to realize that sin leads us to the lowest places. Coming face-to-face with sin is ugly—totally not fun. But we have to step out of the sin to truly step up to the worthy walk with Christ. The Israelites had to step out of Egypt before they could step into the Promised Land.

Sadly, the children of Israel did it the hard way. Because they just couldn't trust God completely, they left Jewish footprints all over that desert for forty years.

Sometimes we do it the hard way too. But do you know what it really takes to head in the right direction? One step. There's one step between sin and the worthy walk, between Egypt and the Promised Land, between slavery and freedom. It's a step of surrender. It's a step of turning. Confessing sin and realizing our unworthiness takes us to the worthy walk of sweet closeness with the Lord.

Where Am I? Who Am I?

So we have to ask ourselves the question, "Where am I?" Stuck in Egypt making bricks? Wandering in the wilderness because of a lack of trust and dependence on the Lord? Or in the Promised Land? Do you know how indescribably sweet it is to step into that Promised Land? It's the place where Jesus is your all. It's that place where you can daily surrender every worry, every care, every struggle.

He wants more than a sinless life from you. He wants to be with you—to help you resist temptation, to give you power to say no to sin. Romans 6:6 spells it out: "For we know that our old self was crucified with him so that the body of sin might be done away with, that we should no longer be slaves to sin." That power to say no to sin comes from him! Your Savior wants to protect you, to walk with you, to love you every minute of every day.

Are you aching to have freedom from sin and a new closeness to your heavenly Father in those higher places with him? Are you just dying to step out of the slavery and darkness of Egypt and roll full speed on all wheels into the blessed sunshine of the Promised Land? Take the step. Name the sin. Don't just hint around—call it what it is. It's ugly, and it's that ugliness that's holding you down, keeping you from stepping up to higher places and a sweet oneness with your God.

Take the Victory Lap!

Do you really believe God can give you victory? Maybe this is a good time for us to remember that it was unbelief that sent the Israelites wheeling on that forty-year errand. Don't step out of slavery only to step into several laps around a desert track. Even if you've struggled with a sin for a long time, believe that he can give you the victory. He can free you. He has the power. He can scrub away the stench of sin and make your life new—better and fresher than any car deodorizer you've ever sniffed. He wants you free.

Your heavenly Father doesn't want you to merely "get used to" living a mediocre life of just getting by spiritually. He wants you to be free and gloriously joyful. He wants you to take a ride with him, as it were—to be close.

Don't be satisfied with a sometimes kind of walk. Sometimes feeling close, sometimes feeling as if he couldn't be farther away. The "one step" it takes to get to that closeness is a big one. It's giving all. You have to be willing to say to him, "I hate my sin. I hate everything that keeps me distant from you. You have all power. Clean me up by that power." Name what it is you want him to cleanse. Ask him to help you stay clean by his power. Make your prayer something like this: "Take away anything and everything that would separate me from you. Empty me of sin and self and fill me up with you. I want to walk with you every second of every day."

What power there is in that prayer! If you pray that prayer from your heart with every ounce of strength and resolve you have, you just might find yourself looking down at your feet only to find them planted smack-dab in the middle of the Promised Land. It's a place of sweet closeness—milk and honey you get to enjoy sitting at the table with the Father who loves you. And yes, I said "milk"—not anything even close to sour cheese.

As for my family and our continuing trek in our cheese-mobile, we've made a few observations along the road. Driving with the windows down in a cute little sports car? Cool. Driving with the windows down in a reeking minivan? Not so cool. We're still just this side of cool.

> Do not let sin control the way you live; do not give in to its lustful desires. Do not let any part of your body become a tool of wickedness, to be used for sinning. Instead, give yourselves completely to God since you have been given new life. And use your whole body as a tool to do what is right for the glory of God. Sin is no longer your master, for you are no longer subject to the law, which enslaves you to sin. Instead, you are free by God's grace.
>
> *Romans 6:12–14 NLT*

step off, girlfriend! 8

The high heels were off. I slid them under my computer desk so I could get some serious work done. My husband was doing some studying at home and the weather was gorgeous, so he opened up the back door for some fresh air. But the puppy totally didn't get the screen door thing. She kept trying to run outside, doing a full-speed face-plant against the screen. So to keep her from straining herself through the giant colander, Richie opened the screen too.

Everything was fine until he finished his studying and headed out—without closing the door. I was working away at my computer when I heard the disturbing sound of a bird slamming itself against the window. Then I heard it again. Then again. When our two cats started going berserk, I realized the thing was not slamming itself on the outside to get in, it was on the inside trying to get out!

I called my husband's office to tell him there was a bird inside my house. And that I had really enjoyed living in this house. And how much I was going to miss it. He wasn't in the office but his secretary had a good laugh.

There was no way I could live with the bird all afternoon. I finally realized that if I wasn't really going to move out (and it took awhile to make that decision), the bird encroacher was going to have to go. The dog and the two cats were all too willing to help me catch the thing, though I don't think they were looking to set it free. The dog thought it was a cool new chew toy, and the cats were sending sinister looks at each other, then back at the bird. I think each was trying to get dibs. They glanced over at me a couple of times, too, as if to thank me for the exceptionally fresh hors d'oeuvre.

A Total Circus

We have atrium windows at the back of our house. That poor bird was so confused. Two stories of humongous, edge-to-edge windows and still no way out. I opened the highest window I could get to and, with broom in hand, proceeded to try to sweep the thing out the open window. I would give the bird a swoop with the broom, then a swoop to each of the other animals to get them to stop trying to help me. I think it must've looked like a lion-taming act gone bad. What a circus. All I needed was a little car with too many clowns in it. A three-ring circus was anything but what I had planned for the day. I wanted to put my heels back on and take a long lunch at some cute and distant café.

One of the most frustrating parts was watching the goofy bird slam itself into any window but the open one. I thought he had died at one point—and I know nothing whatsoever about bird CPR. I did know, however, that mouth to beak was completely out of the question. The bird must've splatted himself against the windows one time too many and completely rattled his little birdie brain. He just fell over, birdie feet sticking up in the air. We're a family of seven, so I never considered "bird under glass" for dinner—even though he had thoroughly tenderized himself. I was just about ready to find a little birdie lily to put on his chest when he revived (which, incidentally, startled me near the point of needing CPR myself).

I'm not sure if the persistent bird had some foul (fowl?) secret plan to blast his way through a closed window or if he was simply not too bright. I'd like to give him the benefit of the doubt, but either way, how good a plan could it have been if he ended up tenderized and pancaked against a window?

Half an hour or so later, I finally managed to give the crasher the heave-ho out the window. The cats were sorely disappointed. I think they sulked all afternoon—although how can a person really tell if a cat is sulking?

Spiritual Head-Smacking

The whole bird-herding incident made me wonder how many times I've frustrated my heavenly Father that same way. He opens a beautiful window, but I smack my head against every closed one instead. I wonder how many gentle "broom nudges" he's sent my way that I've fluttered and fought. We're instructed in Ephesians

5:17, "Therefore do not be foolish, but understand what the Lord's will is." Trying to find my own way is head-smashing foolishness. The next verse tells us to be filled with the Spirit—allowing him to influence our every thought and action, letting his way become our way. Being filled with his Spirit and lining up our lives with his Word is the only real way to get rid of unnecessary fluttering, fighting, and face-smacking folly.

Speaking of folly, what is it that makes me think I can choose the right flight pattern or the right high-heeled steps anyway? I really do need to tell myself to "step off"! That kind of thinking is foolish and prideful. The Lord is the one who determines which step to take and in what kind of shoe. He decides which window is best for me, and he knows just the way I should fly through. Proverbs 16:9 says, "We can make our plans, but the LORD determines our steps" (NLT).

We may make our plans for life—plans that may or may not include a circus. But we find wisdom and spiritual understanding in humbling ourselves and realizing we don't know the right direction on our own. But he does. Being led to higher places is having wisdom and spiritual understanding about who we really are—and that brings humility. The worthy walk is a humble walk. "The humble He guides in justice, and the humble He teaches His way" (Ps. 25:9 NKJV). Want his guidance and his teaching, his wisdom and spiritual understanding? It comes through humility.

Humbly Confident

In Colossians 2:2–3, Paul says,

My goal is that they will be encouraged and knit together by strong ties of love. I want them to have full confidence because they have complete understanding of God's secret plan, which is Christ himself. In him lie hidden all the treasures of wisdom and knowledge.

NLT

Did you notice that in verse 2 we're told that knowing Jesus gives us confidence? I love it that Christ can use our humility to give us confidence! Humble confidence? Only God could make that work! And he does. He makes it work in a way that knits us together. Humble confidence helps us love each other with a more complete, God kind of love.

Colossians 2:2 tells us there's a secret plan. It's not a blast-your-way-through-a-window kind of secret plan. It's a plan for true freedom. Not only does the verse tell us there's a secret, but then it tells us what the secret is! Secret plan revealed: Christ himself.

What woman doesn't love a secret? This is one we can proudly tell—in the most humble way.

This is what the LORD says: Heaven is My throne, and earth is My footstool. What house could you possibly build for Me? And what place could be My home? My hand made all these things, and so they all came into being. [This is] the LORD's declaration. I will look favorably on this kind of person: one who is humble, submissive in spirit, and who trembles at My word.

Isaiah 66:1–2 HCSB

"so that you may walk
worthy of the Lord,
fully pleasing to him"

there was an old woman who lived . . . *where?*

Why would a woman ever live in a shoe? An apartment? Sure. Nice place in the country? I get that. A homey spot in the city or in a nice subdivision? Love it. But a shoe? I never really understood that woman-in-the-shoe nursery rhyme. Cute shoes are meant for an adorable look—not a domicile.

Who in the world would've cast off a shoe big enough to live in, anyway? And let's say there was some giant in town who was willing to donate a shoe. Why wouldn't he go ahead and give the old woman both of them? It's not like he could go about his giant business with only one shoe. Why not give the lady the pair? Maybe she could've turned the other one into a pool house or something.

I wonder how many times the old woman thought about moving, only to be thoroughly frustrated by the real estate nightmare of selling a shoe. How would she ever get an agent to list her property?

Can you imagine her pitch? "We'd like to list our home. It's in move-in condition from heel to toe. You might say it's a multi-level home. There's a lovely view out each eyelet. Incidentally, we replaced the laces last spring and gave the entire outside a good polishing." Maybe if she added, "No need to worry about cedar, brick, or siding. This baby is all leather."

Do we even need to wonder what an inspection disaster there would be? Where would an inspector even begin? Stick out your tongue and say "ah"? The poor woman would probably be saddled forever with the same old shoe. What a tragedy—you know how we women hate to stay stuck in the same old shoe. She didn't even get to change shoes with the seasons!

Oh well, in season and out of season, at least it would be easy enough to give directions to her house. "It's the first high-top on the right." It's always good to know you have the right shoe at the right time.

Right Shoe, Wrong Shoe

I know this next story is terrible, but it really does help illustrate a point, so please forgive me. A few years ago I attended a funeral for one of our church members. I was sitting with my friend Debbie, one of the associate pastors' wives. We were sitting in a long row of staff and staff wives—a pew full of the spiritual pillars of our church. As my husband was speaking, Debbie gave me a little elbow nudge and whispered, "Guess whose husband needs to put a new lightbulb in the closet." Then she sat back and held up her feet. One navy shoe, one brown shoe! One with a little buckle, one with a giant bow! I thought I was going to fall off the pew!

It's bizarre enough when shoes don't match an outfit, but when the shoes don't match each other? Now that was funny!

Being the mature Christian that I am, I totally ignored the fact that I was at a funeral, elbowed the children's director sitting on the other side of me, and whisper-laughed, "Cindy. Get a load of Debbie's shoes." If I was going down in giggle flames, I was taking her with me. There was a little gasp, another elbow to her other side, a few more gasps and elbowing, until pretty soon, the church leadership pew had dominoed into an entire row of stifled guffaws. The pillars were rumbling.

It's not an easy maneuver, the stifled guffaw. Heads were bowed, hands subtly covered the smiles, collective shoulders convulsed up and down, laugh-tears flowed. Somehow, however, we mis-leadingly appeared so reverent that the widow told Debbie after the service that she was deeply touched at how moved we all were. She thought we were crying! Debbie just hugged. What could she say? "Oh, we were moved, alright." What could she do (besides hugging the sweet lady and making a mental note to get her husband to change that closet lightbulb)?

Twinkle Toes to Match Your Clothes

It's wacky when shoes don't match each other. Wacky, too, when you find yourself crying laugh-tears at a funeral—not exactly the appropriate response for the occasion.

And it's wackier still when our knowledge doesn't quite match up with appropriate responses to that knowledge. The "wisdom and spiritual understanding" kind of knowledge from the last section is not enough. As a matter of fact, knowledge alone can be a little dangerous. First Corinthians 8:1 tells us that "knowledge puffs up." Responding to our humble Savior in that kind of puffy pride is about as mismatched as we can get.

Knowledge, wisdom, and spiritual understanding need to be attached to humble, passionate devotion. Why do we want the wisdom and spiritual understanding, the knowledge of godly things Colossians 1:9 refers to? Verse 10 gives us the "so that" that answers this question. It's *so that* we can walk worthy of the

Lord and fully please him—passionately desiring the worthy walk, desperately depending on him for the strength for every step.

Walking worthy hinges on an understanding that God must have the place of supremacy in our lives. It's not about telling God what I can do for him. That's as mismatched with a truly surrendered worthy walk as a blue shoe–brown shoe combo. No match there. And the right walk has to do with understanding that apart from him, I have absolutely nothing to offer.

We have to understand that God is our one true need. Drawing close to him is the most intense and basic necessity of our lives. Passionately drawing close to him is building a strong soul and a worthy walk, living in constant connection, in sweet fellowship with the Father. Higher! And perfectly matched with what he desires for us!

Where Can We Find Passion?

Because we need that constant connection, we need to begin each day by coming into his presence in worship and prayer and by taking the time to let him influence our lives through his Word and by his presence.

Set aside a time to meet with your Father. Passionately draw near to him. It's glorious when we suddenly find that as we draw near to him, he's already drawing near to us! "Draw near to God and He will draw near to you" (James 4:8 NKJV).

Amazing. Even as we're realizing how very unworthy we are to draw near to him, that's the moment he is especially near. The worthy walk in closeness with him is not just about me wanting to have that closeness with him. He wants to have that close and sweet fellowship with me! In my own time with him, I'm sometimes made so clearly aware of that fact that it's almost overwhelming. Almost unbelievable. Certainly unbelievably wonderful.

Take as much time as you need to get to that place of closeness with God. He's waiting every day to make himself known to you. Wait for him, pray and worship him. He is near—and he wants you to know that.

Walkin' the Walk

The worthy walk is not really about the shoes—whether you're trying to match them or trying to sell them as real estate. The Bible often mentions our "walk." When we read about our walk in God's Word, it's about being rooted in him as we live our lives day by day. "As you therefore have received Christ Jesus the Lord, so walk in Him, rooted and built up in Him and established in the faith, as you have been taught, abounding in it with thanksgiving" (Col. 2:6–7 NKJV).

A worthy walk is one that matches up with who we are in Christ. To walk worthy is to passionately be whatever the Lord wants us to be, to passionately do whatever the Lord wants us to do—and to do it all for his pleasure and through his empowering.

Don't you just love the thought of your Father finding pleasure in your walk?

And honestly, he doesn't give the slightest thought to your buckles and bows.

And so, dear brothers and sisters, I plead with you to give your bodies to God. Let them be a living and holy sacrifice—the kind he will accept. When you think of what he has done for you, is this too much to ask? Don't copy the behavior and customs of this world, but let God transform you into a new person by changing the way you think. Then you will know what God wants you to do, and you will know how good and pleasing and perfect his will really is.

Romans 12:1–2 NLT

10

don't try walking with your shoes on the wrong feet

Now that my kids are teenagers, they hardly ever put their shoes on the wrong feet anymore. But it used to be a way of life. I worried when they were younger that their feet might accidentally start curving in the wrong direction. You'd think that the law of averages would dictate them putting their shoes on the right feet around 50 percent of the time, but no such mathematical happenings. I remember telling Andrew for about the third or fourth time in one day that his little Velcro shoes were on the wrong feet when he was around three. He responded, "But, Mom. These are the only feet I have."

A decade and a half or so later, my teens don't put their shoes on the wrong feet, but they don't necessarily put their shoes in the right place either. Once they toss the shoes off their feet, they seem to stick wherever they land.

I was walking through the family room the other day, getting ready to vacuum, and stubbed my toe on Andrew's size 12s (no Velcro anymore), then promptly tripped into Allie's 6s. I surveyed the room. There were at least three shoes for every family member—how we ended up with odd numbers is yet another mystery. You should've seen me trying to vacuum through all that. I was maneuvering through a shoe minefield.

The shoes weren't the only problem. I had to have a little wrestling match with my vacuum cleaner through the whole process. It was doing the wimpy-suction thing—you know, where you get down on your hands and knees and hand-feed it every little fuzz ball and potato chip crumb? If I'm going to do that, I might as well not have a vacuum cleaner. I could just work my way through the shoes to pick up the fuzz and chips and throw them in the trash myself, couldn't I? Cut out the middle man.

Suck-o-rama Mamma

The vacuum had lost all its suckocity. So I got it in a headlock and looked underneath to find out why. I found a little piece of a sock, a length of yarn that could've been an entire sweater in another life, a hunk of rug from the kids' bathroom, and a bunch of those little plastic price tag things that no one ever seems to get all the way into the trash can. No wonder the machine didn't want to work! If all that stuff doesn't affect a vacuum's suction, I don't know what will.

At least it gave me a little reminder. When we let our minds suck up the wrong things, we can't expect them to work the way they're supposed to. We can't expect to walk worthy or to be able to get to higher places. There's so much garbage on TV, in magazines—everywhere. If we let our minds suck up trashy junk, we shouldn't be surprised when we have a hard time dwelling on the things that take us to higher places. This is one mamma who doesn't want her kids' minds or her own mind sucking up the wrong stuff.

We're told in Philippians 4:8 what kind of things we're supposed to think about: "Finally, my friends, keep your minds on whatever is true, pure, right, holy, friendly, and proper. Don't ever stop thinking about what is truly worthwhile and worthy of praise" (CEV). There's a lot less wrestling with our minds when we remember to fill them with the right things.

Point Your Toes

It really is difficult to walk with our shoes on the wrong feet. And sometimes I have trouble even when each shoe is exactly where it's supposed to be. But try walking backward in a pair of high heels. That's asking for trouble. To walk worthy, we have to move forward. Paul tells us in Philippians 3:12–14 to move ahead, forgetting what's behind us:

> Not that I have already obtained all this, or have already been made perfect, but I press on to take hold of that for which Christ Jesus took hold of me. Brothers, I do not consider myself yet to have taken hold of it. But one thing I do: Forgetting what is behind and straining toward what is ahead, I press on toward the goal to win the prize for which God has called me heavenward in Christ Jesus.

May I also encourage you not to let the rotten things that have happened to you in your past keep you in victim mode? Deal with those things, forgive where you need to forgive, get counseling from a godly person you respect if you need to, then look to Christ and look to the future.

The only way to accomplish the purposes God has called you to, and the only way to go deeper with him, is to free yourself from the trappings of the past that stifle you, hinder you, and get you off track. Don't let your past trip you or trap you. Don't let guilt over past sin keep you from moving ahead in your walk with Christ. Once you've dealt with a sin, confessing it and turning from it, accept the forgiveness God offers. It's complete. Free yourself from sin and from hanging onto offenses of the past, point those toes forward, and let your high heels take off toward high places in the renewed strength God gives you.

Getting Your Feet on Track

"Look straight ahead, and fix your eyes on what lies before you. Mark out a straight path for your feet; then stick to the path and stay safe. Don't get sidetracked; keep your feet from following evil" (Prov. 4:25–27 NLT).

Sidetracked? Feet feeling a little unsteady? Don't worry. Your all-powerful God will steady you. That's just what he wants to do. Cry out to him. He longs to answer. In Psalm 40, David reminds us that our Father will lift us up to those high places when we cry out to him, and that he will point us in the right direction, set our "feet on a rock," and give us "a firm place to stand."

> I waited patiently for the LORD to help me, and he turned to me and heard my cry. He lifted me out of the pit of despair, out of the mud and the mire. He set my feet on solid ground and steadied me as I walked along. He has given me a new song to sing, a hymn of praise to our God. Many will see what he has done and be astounded. They will put their trust in the LORD.
>
> Psalm 40:1–3 NLT

Toes forward, let's deal with the past in a healthy way, plant our minds on the things that are worthwhile and praiseworthy, and take off to higher places with the right shoe on the right foot, left shoe on the left foot. Sounds a little like a game of Twister, doesn't it? Only every time you spin, the arrow points forward. It points to Jesus!

> I'm not saying that I have this all together, that I have it made. But I am well on my way, reaching out for Christ, who has so wondrously reached out for me. Friends, don't get me wrong: By no means do I count myself an expert in all of this, but I've got my eye on the goal, where God is beckoning us onward—to Jesus. I'm off and running, and I'm not turning back. So let's keep focused on that goal, those of us who want everything God has for us. If any of you have something else in mind, something less than total commitment, God will clear your blurred vision—you'll see it yet! Now that we're on the right track, let's stay on it.
>
> *Philippians 3:12–16 Message*

11
scratching where it itches with athlete's foot

I think I know why we don't regularly see kids in high heels. It's because kids are constantly running. High heels and speed aren't exactly well suited to each other. Getting from point A to point B when you're a kid seems to always call for extreme velocities. As a matter of fact, kids almost always have to be forced to walk.

I'm not sure exactly when it changes, but I know it does. Suddenly we find ourselves having adjusted our speed entirely. As we near adulthood, not only do we dislike running everywhere, we dislike running anywhere. We don't want to run from point

A to point B. Most of the time, we don't even like to walk there (thus the invention of the remote control). We know we've fully reached adulthood when we have to join health clubs that will force us to run.

Sometimes a Worthy Walk Is a Sprint

But as adults, we need to start running in a whole new way. When there's a temptation, there's one choice: run. We need the good kind of athlete's foot. Being spiritually fleet-footed will scratch where it itches when it comes to fighting sin and walking worthy. Our intentions to do the right thing don't always count. Even Paul struggled. He said in Romans 7:21–25,

> It seems to be a fact of life that when I want to do what is right, I inevitably do what is wrong. I love God's law with all my heart. But there is another law at work within me that is at war with my mind. This law wins the fight and makes me a slave to the sin that is still within me. Oh, what a miserable person I am! Who will free me from this life that is dominated by sin? Thank God! The answer is in Jesus Christ our Lord.
>
> NLT

There's the struggle: sin. And there's the answer: Jesus Christ our Lord!

Sexual sin needs to inspire new speed too. Sprinting to Jesus! First Corinthians 6:18 says, "Run away from sexual sin! No other sin so clearly affects the body as this one does. For sexual immorality is a sin against your own body" (NLT). We need to grow up into mature adults, but that sometimes means we need to remember how to run like a kid.

If there's a temptation taunting you on the Internet, don't determine to fight in your own strength. You need to run by unplugging until you have some accountability or a workable filter. If you're tempted when you find yourself under the influence of a certain person, you need to run by taking yourself out from under that influence. If you're tempted to have inappropriate feelings for someone, you need to run by never allowing yourself to be alone with that person and by never sharing the kind of intimate conversations that should only happen between a husband and a wife. Don't try to find a shortcut button. There's no remote. Whatever it takes, run.

Don't Try Standing Alone

First Corinthians 10:12–13 says,

Even if you think you can stand up to temptation, be careful not to fall. You are tempted in the same way that everyone else is tempted. But God can be trusted not to let you be tempted too much, and he will show you how to escape from your temptations.

CEV

This is one time you don't want to stand alone. Even if you think you can stand up to the temptation, none of us is immune to a fall. Not one of us. Depend on the faithful God who will always provide a way of escape. He promises he'll give us a way to run. When he does, let's tie on those track shoes and take off. Point B? Victory!

The writer of Hebrews says we should "strip off every weight that slows us down, especially the sin that so easily hinders our progress. And let us run with endurance the race that God has set before us" (Heb. 12:1 NLT). How can we do that? The next verse tells us! "We do this by keeping our eyes on Jesus, on whom our faith depends from start to finish" (v. 2).

The enemy would love to see you weighted down and tangled up in a sinful thought life, a judgmental spirit, an immoral act, a self-centered existence, or a gajillion other sins. But not Jesus. He wants you to be light as a feather—free! Stay free by keeping your eyes on Jesus. Don't let that sin nab you and ensnare you. Run, and let Jesus keep you free.

Check Your Speed

If you want to go higher places, if you're longing for a better life, and if you're wondering why you're tangled in a frustrating low life, check your speed. Maybe you're not running when you should be. Allowing sin to have free rein causes a tangled mess. It ends up trapping you every time. It becomes your ruler. If you're allowing your own desires to rule you and trusting in your own power to make you a good person and to allow you to do the right things, you will not find higher places. You won't find goodness on your own.

The highest place—that better life—comes to every person who will not only run away from sin, but to every person who will run to Jesus. Tangled? Let him free you! The healthy high life is the worthy walk of obedience.

Wall-to-Wall Obedience

Doing the healthy thing isn't always doing the thing that looks to be the most fun. I've been trying to eat healthier, for instance.

As part of the new regimen, I tried a protein shake for breakfast. Oh my goodness! Have you ever tasted liquid carpet? This stuff coated every molar in a weird wall-to-wall sort of way. For the longest time I felt like I needed to shave my tongue. Sticking to a healthier diet doesn't necessarily have to come with a hairy tongue, does it?

Sticking to the high life of a worthy walk doesn't have to be hairy either. We need to draw our nourishment not from every trendy new diet or every latest fad but straight from Christ himself. Look again at Colossians 2:6–7:

> And now, just as you accepted Christ Jesus as your Lord, you must continue to live in obedience to him. Let your roots grow down into him and draw up nourishment from him, so you will grow in faith, strong and vigorous in the truth you were taught.
>
> NLT

Drawing nourishment from Christ is nothing like drinking carpet. There's real refreshment in that higher and deeper life. There's growth there, growth in faith, the passage tells us. There's spiritual vigor and vitality—all without the Astroturf aftertaste.

Let's live in obedience, running at the right time, drinking in the right things, with our roots firmly planted in Jesus. That's the kind of spiritual diet we need to stick to if we want divine health.

On the physical health side, I'm sure running wouldn't hurt there either. But if you decide to try one of those protein shake diets, watch out for rug-burn.

The One who is highly honored lives forever. His name is holy. He says, "I live in a high and holy place. But I also live with anyone who turns away from his sins. I live with anyone who is not proud. I give new life to him. I give it to anyone who turns away from his sins."

Isaiah 57:15 NIrV

keep on walking   12

Back to exercise class. Again. I guess I don't need to tell you I'm not the most consistent exercise class attendee on the planet. Not even in the county. Okay, not even in my household. In the class, out of the class. In, out. At least that sounds a little like exercise. The employees know me at almost every shoe store in the entire mall. But the exercise class instructor? I was back again, but she raised one eyebrow and gave me the "And you are . . . ?" look.

Obviously, we weren't off to the best start (or re-restart). It went quickly downhill when she told everyone in the class to get one of the giant balls at the back of the room. Before I knew it, I was on a roll—but it was definitely NOT a good roll. I could tell I was getting on the nerves of the gal exercising next to me about the third or fourth time I all but mowed the poor thing over.

The giant ball thingy had a mind of its own. It seemed determined to escape my grasp. Or maybe the ball was trying to start a fight. It kept slapping me around, then getting away from me, and then smacking that same girl (who has never exercised beside me again, by the way). Somewhere around her third smack (it got her right upside her cute little headband), I started to worry that, if this giant ball didn't beat the tar out of me, then cute sweatband-girl would.

We were supposed to lie across the ball, belly down with our palms on the floor in front of us, then walk our hands out so that just the tops of our legs were balancing on the ball. Hand walking! What kind of high heels would I wear for that?

I would get about to the thighs, totally lose control, and then I would have to scramble up and sprint after my smart-aleck ball. I don't know what everyone got so upset about. It's not like I was TRYING to bowl all their water bottles over. Besides, don't we have screw-on caps for water bottles for just these kinds of happenings?

Painful to the Core

On the upside, there were lots of life lessons all along the way in the fitness class. Of course, I can't think of any of them that weren't pretty painful. But at one point, the instructor said something that I thought was very interesting. She said it during one of my scrambles—and she managed to say it without looking directly at me the entire time she was talking. I had to admire her for that. She said that when our body's core is strong, we have good balance. Let's face it; my inner core is pretty pathetic. There are muscles in there, I'm almost sure, but they're so buried under all those layers of doughnuts and cheesy nachos that I'm doubting I'll ever find them.

I do, however, want it to be very different in the spiritual heart of who I am. I want to always strive to become stronger at the core of everything that truly makes me tick. When life seems all out of balance and I'm rolling this way and that, the first thing I need to ask myself is, how's my core? I need to ask myself what's going on in the very heart of who I am. The shape of my heart will determine whether my walk is worthy or unworthy, successful or unsuccessful, fruitful or fruitless.

What is it that makes a solid spiritual core and a worthy walk? It's that surrender. It's obedience. It's living God's way, fully pleasing him.

Fully Pleasing Me? Others?

Do you ever feel like no matter how you walk, you're not doing it right? You have your Bible study or prayer time, but then later you find someone else's outline (maybe even mine) and you feel like if you didn't do it just the way the latest plan charts it all out, you couldn't possibly have done it the right way?

Let's keep in mind who it is we're seeking to please. Colossians 1:10 reminds us that it's our Father we should strive to please. What kind of fruit really pleases him? What is it that gives us core strength? What is it that he wants from us?

No complicated plan. He makes it simple: "No, O people, the LORD has already told you what is good, and this is what he requires: to do what is right, to love mercy, and to walk humbly with your God" (Mic. 6:8 NLT). Do right, love mercy, and walk humbly. With him every step of the way. Don't let others add so many "requirements" to your worthy walk that they frustrate you right out of your heels until you feel like quitting. Take suggestions in growing in Christ, but focus on what the Father requires.

Even though I'm not the most consistent in attending the exercise class (for which the instructor and most of the class are quite thankful), I want to be completely consistent on the spiritual side. I don't want to merely walk worthy. I want to keep on walking worthy. Not quitting—being "fully pleasing to him" by doing things his way with his requirements. Not my own and not anyone else's.

Galatians 5:22–23 in *The Message* tells us what living God's way brings:

> But what happens when we live God's way? He brings gifts into our lives, much the same way that fruit appears in an orchard— things like affection for others, exuberance about life, serenity. We develop a willingness to stick with things, a sense of compassion in the heart, and a conviction that a basic holiness permeates things and people. We find ourselves involved in loyal commitments, not needing to force our way in life, able to marshal and direct our energies wisely.

Walking worthy brings the tasty life-fruit we get to examine in the next section. It's the kind of fruit that is delightful to the core!

Keep the Ball Rolling

Don't think I didn't notice that Paul says that when we're walking worthy, we're able to "marshal and direct our energies wisely." Maybe a strong physical core and a strong spiritual core are more related than I think.

Keeping at it is essential, spiritually. I need to "keep the ball rolling," as it were. Galatians 6:9 says, "So we must not get tired of doing good, for we will reap at the proper time if we don't give up" (HCSB).

Again in 2 Thessalonians 3:13, we see, "And as for you, brethren, do not become weary or lose heart in doing right [but continue in well-doing without weakening]" (AMP). No weakening! We need to walk the worthy walk and keep on walking it, never quitting.

Of course, being more consistent in the exercise class certainly wouldn't hurt me either. And who knows, if I can keep it up without quitting, maybe I can even get to a place where I walk into the room without everyone grabbing their water bottles.

For, the training of the body has a limited benefit, but godliness is beneficial in every way, since it holds promise for the present life and also for the life to come.

This saying is trustworthy and deserves full acceptance. In fact, we labor and strive for this, because we have put our hope in the living God, who is the Savior of everyone, especially of those who believe.

Be conscientious about yourself and your teaching; persevere in these things, for by doing this you will save both yourself and your hearers.

1 Timothy 4:8–10, 16 HCSB

part 4

"bearing fruit
in every good work"

step lightly and carry a big purse

It's good to accessorize. After all, what would an adorable pair of high heels be without the right purse? Of course, accessorizing with a cute purse can be quite the challenge for me. For it to contain everything I really want it to, it almost has to be a walk-in purse. My husband once suggested a wheelbarrow.

But because of my "purse-sistence" in loading up the bag with every necessity, there's rarely a need my purse can't fill. Lip need? Got the fix. In fact, I probably have enough assorted cosmetic products in there to do the makeup work for an entire Broadway production. I have credit cards to cover every shoe purchase from any store anywhere in my hemisphere. A cell phone, reading glasses so I can dial the cell phone, and multiple lists of all the people I should've already called on the cell phone—it's all in there.

What's NOT in There?

I have to clean out my purse every few months whether I want to or not. I always know it's time when I can't lift it by myself anymore. Last time I cleaned it, I found a ream of receipts that I'm sure I won't need until I can't find them anymore. I also discovered some nail glue that had oozed out and bonded itself to two of my favorite ink pens. I'm just glad I noticed it before grabbing the pens. Granted, I like the idea of never having to search for something to write with again, but I don't think I'd be any too fond of the nickname "Lady Bic."

I found more pens, some paper clips, a couple of notepads, a handful of tacks, and a flash drive—I discovered I'm practically my own Office Depot. Next door to my Office Depot, I think I could open up a Walgreen's. I seemed to have over-the-counter meds for any physical malady you could think of—even a couple in the canine category.

There were plenty of outdated pictures of all my kids, some outdated coupons (why did I think I needed to keep them once they were expired?), and even some outdated keys. Keys, by the way, are officially outdated when you no longer know what they start up or unlock.

In the oral section of my purse, I found a travel toothbrush, four different flavors of gum, three kinds of mints (happily, all sugar-free), some fruity floss, and several other items that would fit nicely into the category of dental hygiene paraphernalia. Four out of five dentists surveyed would approve my purse for membership in the American Dental Association.

Assorted Fruit

One of the most interesting discoveries in the journey to the bottom of my purse was an apple core that one of my kids must've dropped in there sometime when I wasn't looking. Hey, I wondered what that smell was. I thought I must've picked up an extra-fresh pack of Juicy Fruit. It was "juicy fruit," alright. By the time I found it, it was practically a plant! I'm not quite sure how I feel about a purse that grows its own fruit.

Speaking of growing fruit, there are many different kinds of fruit we can bear on the spiritual side. Don't worry, they're a completely different species of fruit than the one growing in my purse. Spiritual fruit is a natural outgrowth of a worthy walk. An apple core would rarely yield a juicy-fruited plant in the bottom of a purse, but a worthy walk will always produce spiritual fruit. Every time.

The Bible tells us that our worthy walk itself is fruit. It teaches that sharing Christ with others is fruit too. Even our praise is a kind of fruit. "Through Jesus, therefore, let us continually offer to God a sacrifice of praise—the fruit of lips that confess his name" (Heb. 13:15). A fruit-bearing life brings pleasure to our heavenly Father.

Showing loving actions and displaying godly character is fruit too. Galatians 5:22 lists the fruit of the Spirit as "love, joy, peace, patience, kindness, goodness, faithfulness, gentleness and self control." We use all of those in serving others. We're fruit-bearers who follow the example of Christ when we selflessly serve and allow the Holy Spirit to work his fruit out in our lives.

Thankfully, we don't have to strain and work to try to bear his fruit any more than I had to strain to grow the weird plant in the bottom of my purse. If we will obediently dig in to serve, the Holy Spirit will produce the fruit in and through us.

Try Some Mixed Fruit

And it's a multifruity marvel. If there's anything we women love, it's multitasking, right? I'm always amazed at the multilevel multitasking I see at the orthodontist's office, for instance. Have you ever noticed how much a person can get done in the waiting room? All five of my kids have had oodles of orthodontic treatment (thank you for your gasps of concern). That means I've seen it all. I've spied kids doing homework, teachers grading homework, and even a few parents doing their kids' homework.

Do I even need to mention how many cell phones I've seen in there? At least I only have one phone in my purse (I think). I've seen several families in the waiting room who had more phones than they had family members. I've seen lots of computers there too. Didn't I see someone making an eBay bid at the last visit? Someone else was actually working on a book manuscript. Oh wait, that was me.

The kids who weren't doing homework were playing video games. It won't shock you to find that there are always tons more kids playing games than doing homework, will it? How did parents get their kids to head for appointments enthusiastically before video games? Some kids have hit their history-making, all-time-high scores while replacing broken brackets. The games have certainly made a lot of kids smile—and with exquisitely corrected grins, I might add. Bite correction and finger dexterity exercises all in one convenient (if not cost-effective) location.

Life is actually pretty good in the orthodontist's office. Sometimes more fruitful in the multitasking department than a purse full of office supplies.

Growing Even More Fruit

Multitasking is a great concept, isn't it? And how about spiritual multitasking? For instance, did you know we can grow and bear fruit AND help others grow at the same time? Doubly fruity! The apostle Paul taught Timothy in chapter 4 of 1 Timothy to keep on growing in ministry. Then he said to "cultivate these things. Immerse yourself in them. The people will all see you mature right before their eyes! . . . Both you and those who hear you will experience salvation" (vv. 15–16 Message).

Immersing ourselves in the things of Christ will cause us to bear fruit and to grow. And when others see our fruit and watch our growth, they're encouraged to be fruitful and grow along too. It's enough to make you smile from ear to ear—with or without headgear.

The Thessalonians were given an example. Paul said in 1 Thessalonians 1:6–8, "You became imitators of us and of the Lord. . . . And so you became a model to all the believers in Macedonia and Achaia. The Lord's message rang out from you not only in Macedonia and Achaia—your faith in God has become known everywhere." Multicity multifruity!

Let's let the Lord's message ring out. Let's make sure we're modeling faith-building, grin-inducing, purse-overflowing growth. We can watch in amazement as the Lord uses our own spiritual growth to fertilize growth in the lives of others. That's the kind of multitasking that all Christians can sink their teeth into!

We might as well keep up the multitask mania in other areas too. I think we might need to make a few rules at the orthodontist's office, though. As I was leaving the office last time, I saw one lady trying to wheel in her tanning bed. Silly woman. I keep mine in my purse.

May you abound in and be filled with the fruits of righteousness (of right standing with God and right doing) which come through Jesus Christ (the Anointed One), to the honor and praise of God [that His glory may be both manifested and recognized].

Philippians 1:11 AMP

14   fashion footed

It's hard to wear high-fashion high heels if you're not in fairly decent physical condition. It can require stilt-walker balance and tightrope-walker muscle tone to maneuver the most challenging fashion-runway-walker heels. Oh, the heights we'll go to, to be able to hit the heights in heels.

Exercise? We know that's a challenge. Change the diet? Some have even tried that. But I noticed one of the first things people typically advise cutting when switching to a healthier eating style is soft drinks. Oh no, not my soft drinks!

Is it easy to get hooked on those sweet little bubbles, or what? Whether it's the real thing, that frosty mug taste, or you just think you're obeying your thirst, it's easy to get in the habit of the old Dr Pepper slogan "Drink a bite to eat at 10, 2, and 4."

Just in case you're thinking you might be addicted, I'll list a few of the warning signs.

Top Ten Ways to Know You're Hooked on Soft Drinks

10. You list Dr Pepper as your personal physician.
9. You're tempted to take a swig from the cup you left in the car—last Thursday.
8. You have soft drink can indentations on your upper lip.
7. The caffeine buzz has you answering the phone—and it's not ringing.
6. Someone asks you if you have a significant other and you answer, "Mr. Pibb."

5. You consider the cola bean a protein—and you put yourself on a high-protein diet.

4. You think the "surge" protector on your computer is soft drink related.

3. The can recycling plant asks if they can set up a branch office in your garage.

2. You spell physics with an *f* and assume it's a study of soda bubbles.

1. Your kids ask you to teach them how to smash cans on their foreheads just like you do.

Hello, my name is Rhonda Rhea. And I'm a soda-pop-aholic. I'm doing much better since my family did the intervention, but I've often wondered if there are any genetics involved. Do you think I could pass this on to my children?

What Am I Passing On?

Yikes, there really are sounder, healthier things to pass along than soda pop chugging and can crushing. My goal is to have something worthwhile to show the next generation.

Psalm 78:4–7 says,

We're not keeping this to ourselves, we're passing it along to the next generation—GOD's fame and fortune, the marvelous things he has done. He planted a witness in Jacob, set his Word firmly in Israel, then commanded our parents to teach it to their children so the next generation would know, and all the generations to come—know the truth and tell the stories so their children can trust in God, never forget the works of God but keep his commands to the letter.

Message

Following the instructions to tell the stories to future generations—that's one of those ways to bear fruit in every good work as Colossians 1:10 tells us to do. If our children and grandchildren know every brand of soda pop backward and forward, and have all the cartoon character stats down pat, but don't have much trust in God, that's a cue for us to start cultivating more fruit. It's our cue to start telling them more energetically about God's fame and fortune and the marvelous things he has done.

Instead of being hooked on soft drinks, we need to help them learn to be hooked on Jesus. Instead of being hooked on sci-fi, we need to show them by our example how to be hooked on and completely connected to the instruction we find in his Word and the commitment to follow him in fruit-bearing obedience.

Beauty Fruity Feet

We need to share the good news with our children, and we need to share the good news with our friends and neighbors—with our world. I don't want this to be a mere casual mention of bearing fruit through sharing Christ, because I know for a fact that astonishing things happen as we share. And what's a *High Heels* book without a good look at God's description of beautiful feet? "How beautiful on the mountains are the feet of those who bring good news of peace and salvation, the news that the God of Israel reigns!" (Isa. 52:7 NLT).

Beautiful, fruit-bearing, good-news-sharing feet are those that buckle on their heels and take the message of salvation to those who don't know. They are feet that encourage those who know him to grow in their love and devotion to Christ.

It's mind-boggling that while sharing the good news is something we do out of love for God, out of obedience to him, and out of a concern for those who don't know him, the blessing in it all seems to bubble right back around to the one who shares.

What Kinds of Bubbly Blessings?

Sharing the good news builds our faith. It encourages us to hang on to the Lord more completely and to know his Word better. It stirs up our love for him and our love for others. It pulls us into a stronger prayer life. We can even find ourselves ready to give up our own comfort and convenience for the sake of someone who needs to know—we grow in discipline and selflessness.

If you've never shared your faith with anyone, I want you to know that it's more blessed than you can imagine. If you're thinking it's a small thing, you've got the wrong picture altogether. And I can tell you as well that the high life depends on it more than you might guess. Those higher places come as we yield in obedience and as we give this love for him and love for those he has created a prominent place in our hearts. There is incredible blessing in sharing! The higher-places kind of blessing!

You can start down the road of beautiful-footed blessing by simply sharing with someone what Jesus means to you or what he's done in your life. That's good news. It's often exactly what God uses to make people thirsty for him. It's the kind of thirst that a soft drink won't fix, but that Jesus can quench in the most complete way. Colossians 4:5–6 doesn't tiptoe around the issue when it says to "be wise in the way you act toward outsiders; make the most of every opportunity. Let your conversation be always full of grace, seasoned with salt." Trading soda for salt and getting wisdom in the deal? Not a bad exchange. Proverbs 11:30 says, "The fruit of the righteous is a tree of life, and he who wins souls is wise."

It's important to understand that he doesn't need you in the equation to bring a person to himself. He does all the work. But it's your honor when he allows you to participate. He's working in lives all over this world to draw people to himself—and blessing of blessings, he wants to include you! "God has given us the privilege of urging everyone to come into his favor and be reconciled to him" (2 Cor. 5:18 TLB). It's a privilege!

It's also our task. A different version of 2 Corinthians 5:18 uses precisely that word: "Christ changed us from enemies into his friends and gave us the task of making others his friends also" (GNT). It's our privilege and our task.

Stepping Up

You can take the next step in sharing your faith when you share this good news with someone who needs to know: Even though everyone has sinned and a holy God must punish sin, by grace Jesus has died to take the punishment we deserve. When we accept the payment he made on our behalf and ask him to take control of our lives, everything wrong we've ever done is forgiven. We get new life here and now and a future special home in heaven. Jesus died on the cross to pay for our sin, but he rose again, and he's alive to fulfill every promise.

Let someone know they can get in on every promise. As soon as you share, stop and look at your feet. Maybe they won't seem any different to you. Maybe you won't see stilt-walker balance and tightrope-walker muscle tone. But I can guarantee, your heavenly Father will see the sweetest fruity feet, blessed and perfectly beautiful! It just doesn't get sweeter than that—not even with bubbles.

My life is worth nothing unless I use it for doing the work assigned me by the Lord Jesus—the work of telling others the Good News about God's wonderful kindness and love.

Acts 20:24 NLT

get your footing

15

Can you imagine me accidentally going to the weights class instead of the aerobics class? Big mistake for a semi-shriveling woman. I knew for sure just how big a mistake it was when I was leaving and I couldn't lift my car keys. Incidentally, by the next day, not only could I not walk in my high heels, I couldn't bend over to put them on.

The instructor said during the class that we needed to stretch ourselves, and that if we could feel muscles burning, that meant something was happening. Feel burning? I was ready to stop, drop, and roll within the first five minutes. Something was happening, alright. They talked about a session to "weight train"; I experienced more of a personal "train *wreck*."

I'm not so good at stretching myself in the muscle department. These muscles (and I'm using the word "muscles" in its loosest terms) are still a little lazy. When I hear my musclelike parts whine, I'm usually willing to listen—and to give in to them. I've discovered they find great comfort in a good cream-filled chocolate éclair. At least my muscles have exceptional taste.

Feel the Burn

I wonder if I get a little lazy about stretching myself spiritually too. Serving Christ isn't a job for spiritual couch spuds. No, it requires exercising spiritual muscle. It's not always easy. Sometimes we're stretched in new directions as we're "bearing fruit in every good work."

Are you stretching? If you can feel the burn, something is likely happening. Second Timothy 1:6 says, "This is why I remind you to fan into flames the spiritual gift God gave you" (NLT). I hope I'm not reading more into this than I should, but since Paul instructs us to "fan into flames" our spiritual gifts, doesn't that mean that sometimes God gives a gift to us as a spark? If so, how exactly would we encourage that spark to catch on? Fanning it, encouraging it, using it!

Some of us may have spiritual gifts we don't know about because we've never tried them out. We've never fanned the flames. We've never stretched ourselves until we feel the burn.

"A spiritual gift is given to each of us as a means of helping the entire church" (1 Cor. 12:7 NLT). We each have a spiritual gift. According to this verse, that gift has a purpose. Its purpose is to help the church—to serve in the body of Christ. First Peter 4:10 says, "As each one has received a gift, minister it to one another, as good stewards of the manifold grace of God" (NKJV). It's clear. The gifts we have are given by God's grace. And we're not being good stewards of his gracious gifts if we're not using them in fruitful ways to serve one another.

Cues for Living

It's about more than ourselves—the impact of our fruit-bearing service goes even beyond the benefit of the one we're serving. It's a cue to others.

I saw a commercial for cute shoes the other day, and suddenly I needed them. Funny how that works. It works on my kids too. I was working at the computer one evening when I heard a primal kind of yell from the family room downstairs, "I NEED A TOASTER STRUDEL!"

Weird. It was about seven o'clock in the evening and the "strudel alert" was totally out of the blue. I said, "What in the world brought that on?"

One of the kids answered, with great drama, "I'm the victim of a major food cue here—and I have to have the strudel!"

Don't let anyone tell you advertising doesn't work. At another TV food cue the other day, my kids pooled their money for a late-night DQ run. I think they might've dipped into their Christmas savings. Can you imagine my teenagers trading *my* Christmas gifts for some cookie dough Blizzards?

There are especially good, fruitful cues we can give in to, though. It's good to have mentors in the faith—people who faithfully offer us cues in fruitful Christian living. And it's good to mentor others. It's good to let our example of bearing fruit in every good work inspire them to serve too.

"Stooping" to Higher Places

Jesus gives us our ultimate cues for living, of course. We can wholly trust his example. He was an example to his disciples and to us, for instance, when he washed his disciples' feet just before he went to the cross. The Creator of the universe, the King of Kings, stooping to wash his followers' dirty feet. What an amazing scene!

After taking on that servant role, he said, "And since I, the Lord and Teacher, have washed your feet, you ought to wash each other's feet. I have given you an example to follow. Do as I have done to you" (John 13:14–15 NLT).

It's Jesus who gives us a flawless example. He's the one who will never, ever disappoint. But he can also use the testimonies and examples of others to spur us on in service. He can also show us so much through the godly people he brings into our lives. It's good to watch people who unswervingly watch Christ. Sometimes we're the watchers. Sometimes we're the ones showing the examples.

But our service is not merely a "good thing." It's the higher-places life of following the Master. To fully serve him, we simply have to be willing to serve others. And if we really love him, we have to be willing to serve him with everything we've got—every second of every day, every brain cell, every dollar, every ounce of life—every chocolate-éclair-covered muscle. We will never find higher places with him if we neglect to surrender to him in this area of loving service.

Your Fruit Assignment

Did you know he has fruit picked out just for you? He has special good works he picked and planned for you to do. Paul tells us in Ephesians 2:10 that God "has created us for a life of good deeds, which he has already prepared for us to do" (GNT). You have a special assignment from your Maker—it's a calling!

Would you like to go higher places in serving Jesus? Would you like to know what's important to him? This is it! Paul capsulizes it in his prayer:

> I pray that your love for each other will overflow more and more, and that you will keep on growing in your knowledge and understanding. For I want you to understand what really matters, so that you may live pure and blameless lives until Christ returns.
>
> Philippians 1:9–10 NLT

What's important to Jesus? A love that overflows and a love that grows with our growing understanding of how to love him.

Jesus said in John 12:26, "If anyone serves Me, he must continue to follow Me [to cleave steadfastly to Me, conform wholly to My example in living and, if need be, in dying] and wherever I am, there will My servant be also. If anyone serves Me, the Father will honor him" (AMP).

Honor All Around

With serving, following, cleaving, and conforming comes honor. We don't usually think of stooping to wash feet as a place of honor. But Jesus changes the way we think. He takes us to higher places of thinking when we serve, follow, cleave, and conform to him.

Maybe fruitful service is a bit of a stretch for you. Maybe it's something new. Go ahead. Give it a try anyway. Trying new ways to serve can help you discover new and fabulous ways to love the Savior. Fan those flames! Your fruit will glorify your God! "May you always be filled with the fruit of your salvation—those good things that are produced in your life by Jesus Christ—for this will bring much glory and praise to God" (Phil. 1:11 NLT).

I want to find new ways to glorify our amazing God too. I want to try new ways to serve. New ways to serve him are new ways to love him.

Now that I can lift my keys again, I'm heading out. Somewhere along the journey, by the way, I might have to swing through Dairy Queen for a smoothie, but I'm on my way!

> It is God himself who has made us what we are and given us new lives from Christ Jesus; and long ages ago he planned that we should spend these lives helping others.
>
> *Ephesians 2:10 TLB*

---

16 put on your dancing tennies

Picture a graceful dancer gliding across the room. Now picture the opposite, and you'll have an accurate image of that spaniel pup I told you about. She's a girl, but she's anything but ladylike. I just can't see her in high heels of any kind. No sparkles or boa for this dog.

You should've seen what she wore home from the vet's office the other day. You would expect a girl pup to come home in some cute doggy heels—at least some fashion-conscious Hush Puppies. But this one? She came home wearing a cone. Every time I looked at her, it made me want ice cream. A couple of times I caught a glimpse of her out of the corner of my eye and thought my lamp had turned over. On the upside, I think our satellite picked up a much clearer signal when we pointed her east. And she was her own megaphone. At least she had enough fashion sense to look humiliated, the poor thing.

What's in a Name?

What could be more humiliating than the cone? How about discovering you're a dog that's all thumbs—without even having any thumbs? I already told you about the day she was very near to straining herself through the screen door, didn't I? It's a wonder she didn't shove herself clean through that giant grinder and turn herself into a big doggy sausage. What's really funny is that, as awkward as the puppy is, her name is Gracie.

It hasn't been long since we took Gracie in, so we're all still experiencing a lot of puppy transitions. You can't pick up a tennis ball or stuffed animal in our house that doesn't make a slobber-log squishy sound. The entire upstairs smells a little like puppy breath. Every square inch has been sufficiently sniffed, then thoroughly chewed and covered with drool.

It's been an adjustment for all of us in the household, granted, but the biggest adjustment is on the part of the two cats who haven't entirely unpuffed since the pup lumbered through the front door. I think I actually saw Gracie grin when she tried to greet the kitties (even though I'm embarrassed to say the cats did not display good social skills at the meeting at all—hospitality is definitely not their thing). I didn't have a puppy language interpreter, but I could almost hear Gracie saying, "Hey, those look really chewy! I wonder how far that fat one can roll."

Transitional Government

Fortunately for the chewy cats, the puppy seems to think the stairs are some sort of magic portal and won't even go near them. So the downstairs has officially been claimed by the cats, and they're setting up a little kitty kingdom. I think there's a provisional government now in place, and you have to go through Cat Customs and prove you're not even remotely canine to go down there. They're checking IDs.

Speaking of IDs, when we've given our lives to Christ, we become part of his kingdom. Not kitty related. Our identity is in him. And there's no need for a magic portal. We have Jesus! Because we have a new identity in Christ, we're free to bear fruit like we never could before. The worthy walk we're seeking is actually a form of bearing fruit itself. In Romans 6:22, Paul says, "But now having been set free from sin, and having become slaves of God, you have your fruit to holiness, and the end, everlasting life" (NKJV). Do you love the thought of bearing holy fruit?

Paws and Reflect

Think about the life God has given you and the joy there is in loving and serving him. What satisfaction there is in bearing the holy fruit of a worthy walk! Want to go higher? Ask him to make you more like Jesus and to allow you to fulfill his every desire in you. Ask him to bring about the holy fruit he wants for your life. Say to him, "Here I am, Lord—all of me." Know that when you are filled with his Spirit and relying on his power, you can accomplish more than you ever dared dream. All for him! Yield yourself to him, by faith, knowing that he will make happen all the purposes he has for you. It's one of the most glorious aspects of a sweet, close fellowship with him—and it's living out what it means to walk worthy and bear fruit. Christ in you!

As you're praying, watch for signs of anything that would hinder your worthy walk of holiness. Unholiness has a sly way of sneaking in. Wouldn't it be nice if going to those higher places meant we would never struggle with sin again? But we still live in bodies of flesh, and that means that we'll still struggle with that shallow girl in each of us.

Happily, as we're growing in holiness and learning more about the worthy walk, we do sin less. Galatians 5:16 says, "Walk in the Spirit, and you shall not fulfill the lust of the flesh" (NKJV). When we're in tune with the knowledge of his will and we're growing closer to him, understanding more and more what his will is for our lives and how satisfying it is to bear holy fruit, sin loses its appeal.

But the battle isn't over. The next verse in Galatians 5 says, "For the flesh lusts against the Spirit, and the Spirit against the flesh; and these are contrary to one another, so that you do not do the things that you wish" (NKJV).

As we grow closer to him, we see areas of sin in our lives that we never really noticed before. Sin we might have considered "not that big of a deal" before becomes more obvious. When we're striving for clean, holy lives, the darkness of even the smallest sin shows up so much more clearly. The closer we are to him, the more we become aware of our sin.

Aren't you thankful that God doesn't show us every area of sin at one time? How utterly devastating and overwhelming would that be! Mercifully, he more often takes his holy flashlight into our lives. He doesn't flick on the overhead light to show us every area of dirt and clutter. Instead, he shines the flashlight in one corner and says, "There's an area that needs your attention over there." We take care of that area, then he moves the light to another area and says, "Now how about this little mess right here?" He helps us clean an area of inappropriate anger, then when it's all clean in that corner, he shines his light on an ugly attitude of jealousy we didn't even realize we had.

That's growth in the worthy walk. It's seeing his fruit in our lives. Progress in holy fruit is truly one of the most magnificent higher-places happenings in a life.

Gracie Progress?

As far as Gracie-progress goes, we're moving a little more slowly in that area. A couple of nights ago, she found Andrew's huge hot-pink loofah (we'll talk about why my college boy had a huge hot-pink loofah another time—suffice it to say it's one of the big jokes on his college campus).

Andrew had just moved all his things home from college for the summer when Gracie noticed the loofah. I guess she figured Andrew brought it home as a little souvenir for her. By the time we found her, hot-pink fluff covered the entire family room floor. Oh the humanity. Pink loofah carcass everywhere! It looked like someone had plucked a ballerina.

It wasn't a total loss. There was residual shower gel in the loofah, and the family room smells a lot less like puppy breath. Never mind that Gracie is still blowing bubbles.

> You were taught, with regard to your former way of life, to put off your old self, which is being corrupted by its deceitful desires; to be made new in the attitude of your minds; and to put on the new self, created to be like God in true righteousness and holiness.
>
> *Ephesians 4:22–24*

"and growing in the knowledge of God"

a step and a squish   17

It was my little Daniel's nine-month mile marker—certainly an occasion for a trip to the photo studio. I spiffed him up in his most adorable nerd suit, complete with suspenders, bow tie, and white shoes. Talk about cute. I even spiffed myself up. Moms have to look cute on mile-marker days too. So I put on my favorite high heels and headed to the mall with my sweet baby.

The poor baby had a nagging, malicious ear infection that wouldn't let go. But the doctor had pulled out the big guns and put him on one of the more infection-exploding medicines the day before. I was so tickled that even with the ear infection, he was able to muster some cute grins for the camera.

Did Someone Say "Scoop"?

The photographer finished and I scooped Daniel up to go. But I hadn't realized that an infection-exploding antibiotic could also be a diaper-exploding one. "Big guns" was right. We're talking radioactive baby bazooka-britches with major poop-le-ar fallout. I had him perched on my hip, so when the explosion sent waves right out the leg of the diaper, it ran all down my right leg. Before I could do anything, it flowed right into my shoe. Have you ever tried to write a check for baby pictures with a toxic poop river flowing into one of your favorite heels?

I may have overpaid by a few hundred dollars, I'm not sure. I just wanted to get out of there and get home. You should've heard me as I practically sprinted through the mall: step, *squish*, step, *squish*, step, *squish*.

By the time I got to a place where I could change the baby, we both needed a change. Not only did I have to change nearly every piece of clothing I had on, but some of them never recovered. Argh—my favorite shoes.

Jesus brings the most vital changes into our lives in a much tidier way. Everyone who comes to Christ comes as a babe, not knowing much about the walk of faith. But the Bible teaches us that by his grace he begins to change us from the inside out. He transforms us. He makes us look more like himself. Paul said,

> Then we will no longer be like children, forever changing our minds about what we believe. . . . Instead, we will lovingly follow the truth at all times—speaking truly, dealing truly, living truly—and so become more and more in every way like Christ.
>
> Ephesians 4:14–15 TLB

I Never Met a Baby Who Never Needed Changing

To become more like Christ is to become more what we really long to be. It's a "becoming" that is the very road to every high place. I have to confess, though, sometimes changing gets messy. Sometimes changing and growing happens through trials, heartache, or testing. Still, I never met a baby who never needed to be changed.

I'm so glad that my baby never said, "Hey, I like myself this way. I don't need to change." Do you think a baby is happier and more comfortable sitting in the same old diaper, or cleaned up, new and freshly changed?

We wrapped up the last chapter with Ephesians 4:22-24. Let's take another look at Paul's instructions in those verses:

> You were taught, with regard to your former way of life, to put off your old self, which is being corrupted by its deceitful desires; to be made new in the attitude of your minds; and to put on the new self, created to be like God in true righteousness and holiness.

In *Words of God for Young Disciples of Christ*, Andrew Murray said,

> The young Christian must not remain weak; he must grow and increase in grace; he must make progress and become strong. God lays it upon us as a command. His word gives us concerning this point the most glorious promises. It lies in the nature of the thing: a child of God must and can make progress. The new life is a life that is healthy and strong: when a disciple surrenders himself to it, the growth certainly comes.[4]

Hitting the Dusty Trail

"Growing in the knowledge of God" is all part of the higher walk. All through the writing of this book, I've been begging God to grow me and to take me to higher places. I didn't want to just "write a book." Anyone can do that—and most can do it a lot better than I can. So are you wishing I had admitted that on the cover of the book instead of here in the middle when you've already invested time and money in it?

Sorry, but now that you're sort of stuck with me, I want you to know that I didn't take writing a "higher places" book lightly.

And I didn't want to *send* readers on a journey. I wanted to go on a journey, hopefully a shared one—the kind of journey that would bless God. I can't tell you how much time I've spent praying that the Lord would work in my life through this trip. I've asked him to change me. To take me to higher, deeper, richer places of worship and intimacy with him.

Maybe I'm making my asking sound a little more dignified than it's really been. That "asking" mentioned in the introduction has actually been much more like begging. It's been grabbing on to the hem of his robe and refusing to let go until he filled my deepest need: my need for more of him. Picture me as a giant dust mop and you'll have a pretty accurate image of how dignified the whole thing has been.

But it has already been an amazing ride to those higher places I've begged to go. I keep clinging to that hem. I'm picturing a cleaner, freshly mopped trail behind me as I pick a few twigs from between my teeth. I've prayed, "Lord, take me higher," and he has faithfully revealed places in my life where I need to grow. Little pockets of selfishness I was sadly content to ignore. Areas in my life where a lack of discipline has weighed me down. More of me that I needed to surrender. And each time I've caught a little glimpse of what the high life should look like. I've been surprised at how much growing I still need to do. Ouch. Another twig. But through tears and giggles, I'm not letting go. I'm hanging on for dear life. That "dear life" is the treasured, high places life. *Do whatever it takes, Lord, to get me there. Grow me. Change me.*

Practical Growing

We're called to be constantly growing and developing spiritually in some very practical ways. In Acts 2 we're told about the growth of the first-century church. "Those who believed what Peter said were baptized and added to the church. . . . They joined with other believers and devoted themselves to the apostles' teaching and fellowship. . . . They worshiped together" (vv. 41–42, 46 NLT). It's interesting to me that the same things that were encouraged for growth at the very first—teaching, fellowship, and worship—are still important factors in growth today. We need to stay plugged in to a local church body, joining with other believers, working to advance the kingdom.

Let's keep stepping together, allowing Christ to grow us and change us—hanging on to his hem through every step of the adventure. There may be some Galilean dust and a twig or two between the teeth now and then, but what an amazing trip! And honest, there aren't that many steps with squishes.

> Then we will no longer be infants, tossed back and forth by the waves, and blown here and there by every wind of teaching and by the cunning and craftiness of men in their deceitful scheming. Instead, speaking the truth in love, we will in all things grow up into him who is the Head, that is, Christ. From him the whole body, joined and held together by every supporting ligament, grows and builds itself up in love, as each part does its work.
>
> *Ephesians 4:14–16*

lessons for loafers 18

We had a big party at our house a few weeks ago. I really hate to admit to this—especially in writing. It's bound to be used against me at my inevitable sanity hearing. But I burned more calories on my exercise machine while getting ready for that open house than

I have since I bought it. Here's the goofy part. I was wearing high heels. High heel aerobics? Not exactly, because here's the goofier part. I wasn't using the machine to exercise. No, I burned all those calories by PUSHING the monstrous thing into the storage area. Now that's just embarrassing.

Doesn't it seem like simply owning the machine should make me fit? After all, I invested a big hunk of money in it. I'm sure I thought I'd see the muscle multiplying and the fat melting away even as I wrote out the check.

Money Can't Buy Me Fitness

I wonder if there are people who have the same kind of strange ideas when it comes to spiritual issues. Colossians 1:10 tells us we need to be growing in the knowledge of God. Do you suppose some people think that by finding the biggest, fattest, most expensive Bible, they automatically become spiritual? Or maybe they feel that if they learn to pray exactly like every TV evangelist they hear, then they'll have more of God's ear.

But it doesn't work that way. Ephesians 6:17 tells us to "take" the Word of God. Not just buy it. Not set it on a shelf for some kind of spiritual protection. We're not to just glance at a few pages now and then. No, we're to "take the sword of the Spirit, which is the word of God." TAKE it. We're to wield it. How wacky would we consider a soldier who strapped on the heaviest, shiniest sword, then went into battle trying to bop people with its sheath? That would be goofier than trying to exercise by pushing the exercise machine around the room. We would consider that soldier even more destined for a sanity hearing than me!

We can instead use God's Word and continue to grow in it, letting it become more ingrained in what we do and who we are.

It's a big part of what being filled with the Holy Spirit and walking in him is all about. That's when we're able to do what we were designed to do.

No Loafer Zone

In studying his Word and in praying to him too, we can be "growing in the knowledge of God" by going deeper and higher. Maybe you've taken a step. What's your "next, next step"? Are you ready to strap on your high heels and take it? As high heel gals, the last thing we want to be is loafers!

Growing in Studying His Word

Ever feel a little guilty and frustrated when you hear a preacher give a great sermon or a teacher lead some higher places kind of Bible study? We've all been there. We wonder how they got to those higher places through God's Word, and it makes the fact that we don't necessarily know how to get there stand out all the more. It highlights the fact that we spend so many more hours watching TV or reading other things—even reading *about* the Bible more than we actually read the Bible.

We already know we need to study God's Word, but we feel a little clueless and frustrated when we pick it up and don't know where to go. Can we get to those higher places without knowing the Bible more intimately? Can we follow in Christ's footsteps without it? Jesus said, "If you abide in My word [hold fast to My teachings and live in accordance with them], you are truly My disciples" (John 8:31 AMP).

We grow as disciples of Jesus who follow in his footsteps as we discipline ourselves to love and study and obey his Word and make it a consistent part of our daily walk. No need to go to guilt-ridden places. You can grow in your love and consistency in God's Word. Really you can! Pick a book of the Bible and dig in. Find a study resource or two that will help take you to higher places of learning. Then stick with it every day. Finish one study, start the next. You'll never regret time invested in studying the most important, life-changing book of all time.

Growing in Praying to Him

We should always be growing in our prayer lives too. Most of us as children learned to pray sweet but simple prayers. If as adults we're still at "Now I lay me down to sleep," then it's definitely time to move on to some higher prayer places. Time to grow! I love Andrew Murray's classic insights into a growing, higher places prayer life from *With Christ in the School of Prayer*:

> As we grow in the Christian life, the thought and the faith of the Beloved Master in His never-failing intercession becomes ever more precious, and the hope of being like Christ in His intercession gains an attractiveness before unknown. And as we see Him pray, and remember that there is none who can pray like Him, and none who can teach like Him, we feel the petition of the disciples, "Lord, teach us to pray," is just what we need. And as we think how all He is and has, how He Himself is our very own, how He is Himself our life, we feel assured that we have but to ask, and He will be delighted to take us up into closer fellowship with Himself, and teach us to pray even as He prays.[5]

We need to offer ourselves to God as learners—as those who really do desire to go to those higher places. And what better way to step there than in prayer? Prayer is tapping on the door of the Almighty. Even better, it's climbing up onto the lap of a loving Father who loves to hear every word we speak to him. It's tapping into the power he wants to so graciously provide. It's the avenue of blessings he's waiting to grant, promises he's waiting to fulfill—so much power! *Jesus, teach us to pray!*

It's just what the disciples asked. They wanted to go higher places too. Andrew Murray commented further on how Jesus loves to teach us to pray:

> Nothing delights Him more than to find those whom He can take with Him into the Father's presence, whom He can clothe with power to pray down God's blessing on those around them, whom He can train to be His fellow-workers in the intercession by which the kingdom is to be revealed on earth. . . . Jesus loves to teach us how to pray.[6]

Growing in Knowing

"Growing in the knowledge of God" speaks of a specific kind of knowledge. It's not the Greek word for "feelings" but an intimate knowledge of the Father—and there are no higher places without this knowledge. It's time to do our spiritual exercises (no machine required) and to grow in knowledge. First Peter 2:1–3 says, "Therefore, rid yourselves of all malice and all deceit, hypocrisy, envy, and slander of every kind. Like newborn babies, crave pure spiritual milk, so that by it you may grow up in your salvation, now that you have tasted that the Lord is good." He is good! Let's make knowing him and growing in him our deepest life passion, so that we truly can do what we were designed by him to do.

And just so you know (I confess it's out of a little guilt), I'll be dragging my exercise machine back out of storage this week. I guess I'll try a little harder to use it to do what it was designed to do too. Hey, do you think that hauling the thing back out might earn me enough aerobic points to get me through till next summer?

> But grow in the grace and knowledge of our Lord and Savior Jesus Christ. To him be glory both now and forever! Amen.
>
> *2 Peter 3:18*

---

19 some fancy footwork

Cinderella's fairy godmother certainly came up with some very creative ball wear. But I have to question her wisdom with the glass shoe call. Fancy, yes, but what kind of fancy footwork would it take to make sure she didn't crack a shoe?

What was that godmother thinking? One stubbed toe and the night could've ended with a trip to the ER. Sure, it would've been nice not to have to worry about all the messy shoe cleaners or polishes. A few squirts of Windex and they would be streak-free and ready to party. But how carefree could a person be if she had to worry that if her feet started sweating, her prince would wonder why her shoes were fogging up?

Even without the sweat fog, I'm wondering how the shoes could be anything even near comfortable. There's just no give in a glass shoe. If I tried to walk in shoes that didn't bend in any direction whatsoever, I can almost guarantee I would have more of a Frankenstein walk than a princess one.

Crack-a-Toe-a

Dancing with a Frankenstein gait would be problematic enough, but a girl would probably be distracted through the entire dance worrying about serious shoe/foot danger. What if it turned out the prince wasn't the best dancer in the kingdom? Puts a whole new spin on "break dancing," doesn't it? I can envision a different ending to that fairy tale, with Cinderella limping back to her own little corner in her own little chair.

And I don't mean to be critical—especially since the fairy godmother didn't have a lot of raw materials to work with—but couldn't she have done a better job sizing up the shoe situation? How badly would a pair of shoes have to fit for a princess-to-be to run right out of one? Maybe we should give her the benefit of the doubt and assume her wand needed a little recalibrating or something.

But from any and every direction, I'm thinking glass shoes were just not the wisest move.

We probably won't ever be given the task of outfitting pre-royalty in magical party duds. But how can we grow in making the wisest moves in all areas of our real life? Wise moves—all wisdom—is as wrapped up in our obedient surrender to Jesus as the carriage was wrapped up in the pumpkin. Practically the same.

Growing in this knowledge sounds so simple: wise, obedient surrender. You simply say the magic words, "I'm deciding to give you all, Lord," add a little fancy footwork of obedience, and—*bippety-boppety-boo*—wisdom! When a person comes to a higher place of giving more of herself to the King, amazing blessings appear.

What Kind of Crack Is That?

But there are wonderful places to go higher still, as we come to the conclusion that our life and our surrender to God is not about us receiving a blessing. It's about us *becoming* a blessing. It's total surrender of self, self-promotion, self-indulgence, self-centeredness—cracking and stripping away absolutely everything self-related.

For some, the next step in the worthy walk is letting go of making our own plans or choosing our own way and then asking God to tag a blessing on it after it's all said and done. The next step from there is making surrender and obedience part of every decision, every plan, every thought—making it all about his pleasure instead of our own. That's where we find wisdom and growth in the worthy walk. "Finally then, brethren, we urge and exhort in the Lord Jesus that you should abound more and more, just as you received from us how you ought to walk and to please God" (1 Thess. 4:1 NKJV). We grow in living to give him pleasure!

Wisdom comes as we put ourselves entirely in God's hands and under his control. It's coming to him every day, seeking the highest, closest place, saying something like, "Oh Lord, is there anything at all you see in me that doesn't fit with your plan, purposes, and desires for me? Is there any little pocket of anything I've kept to myself? Take it all!"

Jesus's words go to the heart of the matter: "Anyone who holds on to life just as it is destroys that life. But if you let it go, reckless in your love, you'll have it forever, real and eternal" (John 12:25 Message).

At the point of letting go of every ounce of ourselves and clinging single-mindedly to him, our relationship with him is transformed more dramatically than a pumpkin changing into a coach. This is better than magic!

Good-bye, Self—Hello, Higher Places

Without single-minded devotion, our wisdom is wishy-washy—more fragile than a glass slipper—and our lives lack stability. James 1:5–8 says,

> If any of you lacks wisdom, let him ask of God, who gives to all liberally and without reproach, and it will be given to him. But let him ask in faith, with no doubting, for he who doubts is like a wave of the sea driven and tossed by the wind. For let not that man suppose that he will receive anything from the Lord; he is a double-minded man, unstable in all his ways.

> NKJV

As you let go of self and grab on to surrender, you can find a closeness with Christ that will make you look back in amazement that you once settled for what you considered "a good Christian life." You can find yourself miles higher in your worthy walk as you relinquish all in sweet, constant, unbroken fellowship with him.

Guess what you'll find there? Everything. Wisdom? It's there. Love? Acceptance? Fulfillment? All there. You'll catch yourself thinking, "There is nothing more in this world that I want or need than this tight-knit fellowship with my Lord." It's like looking down and suddenly becoming aware of having traded the life of Cinderella rags for the privileged life of a regal princess. You're a daughter of the King!

Fashion Advice, Princess to Princess

On the lighter side, now that we've established ourselves as royalty, maybe we can give some needed fashion guidance to anyone heading out the door in breakable shoes: It just doesn't matter how much they flatter if in a little pinch they're likely to shatter.

MY SON, if you will receive my words and treasure up my commandments within you, Making your ear attentive to skillful and godly Wisdom and inclining and directing your heart and mind to understanding [applying all your powers to the quest for it];

Yes, if you cry out for insight and raise your voice for understanding,

If you seek [Wisdom] as for silver and search for skillful and godly Wisdom as for hidden treasures,

Then you will understand the reverent and worshipful fear of the Lord and find the knowledge of [our omniscient] God.

For the Lord gives skillful and godly Wisdom; from His mouth come knowledge and understanding.

He hides away sound and godly Wisdom and stores it for the righteous (those who are upright and in right standing with Him); He is a shield to those who walk uprightly and in integrity,

That He may guard the paths of justice; yes, He preserves the way of His saints.

Then you will understand righteousness, justice, and fair dealing [in every area and relation]; yes, you will understand every good path.

For skillful and godly Wisdom shall enter into your heart, and knowledge shall be pleasant to you.

Proverbs 2:1–10 AMP

sometimes sandals are the best high heels   20

I confessed my shoe gluttony early in the book. I thought I'd go ahead and get that out of the way and make sure I had no dignity left in that area before we even reached the end of the first section. I'm a firm believer in full disclosure.

But maybe you've been wondering if you're in the shoe-glutton class too. What kind of ministry would this book offer if I didn't give you the warning signs of shoe-aholism?

Ten Ways to Know You're a Shoe-aholic

10. You keep finding shoes you can't remember ever buying.
9. You've mastered the magicians' scarf trick, with a twist—your closet is the sleeve, your shoes are the scarves, and *presto!* you pull out one pair, then another pair, then another . . .
8. You have great accessories, but you can no longer afford food.
7. The city says you have to get a merchant's license if you want to keep that size shoe inventory.
6. Amelda Marcos calls you up to borrow a pair or two.
5. Your friends come over to do a shoe intervention, and when they get to the closet-cleaning part, you notice they brought C-4.
4. As you get the last of your shoes out of the closet to sort them, the echo . . . *echo* . . . *echo* . . . scares out the bats.
3. You lay off the shopping for a couple of weeks and shoe stocks take a dangerous nosedive.

2. You decide to name one of your children Prada.
1. The city declares your closet overflow situation a state of emergency, and they make you wait for the government to send in the relief workers before you can start the cleanup.

I've passed on the shoe-mania gene to my daughters. Allie, for instance, could likely outfit an entire third world village with the shoes she has in her closet. And a scary closet it is.

Kaley is sixteen and she has the mania down pat too. I know dealing with her mania is pretty hypocritical of me, since my closet could make any relief worker throw up his hands and walk out. But Kaley's closet? Positively unsafe! As scary as it was, I decided, hypocrisy or no hypocrisy, if she was ever going to find anything in that closet again, I was going to have to dig in and help her clean it—from the inside. It was either that or toss in a grenade.

I tossed the grenade idea around a little, but I never found an aisle at Wal-Mart marked "Miscellaneous Explosives." Still, the deed had to be done. I went in. Unarmed. Oh, the things a mother must do for the safety of her family!

Mind you, we've only lived in the house for four years. Still, from the look of it, that closet hadn't had a good cleaning for a couple of decades. I thought about the origin of the word *closet*. Isn't it from the Greek "closetorium," which means "where the dog wouldn't even throw up"? I don't think C-4 would've made a dent in this thing.

Tales from the Closetorium

We found broken crayons stuck to an old sucker stick. We were both amazed there was so much stickiness left; it had been at least two years since she'd eaten it. The sucker, not the crayons. It's been at least fourteen years since she's eaten crayons. We found a math paper from third grade, the box from her SpongeBob clock (she didn't have the clock anymore, but she still had the box—go figure), her cheerleading uniform from three years before, and a VCR she had taken apart and couldn't get back together.

But do you know what's worse than six thousand VCR pieces? Eight thousand price tags! It looked like she still had the tags from every item she'd purchased over the last six years. Since we both had to deal with all the tags, did that make it a little like "tag" team closet cleaning?

I wondered if it would've been better to just close the closet door and pretend I didn't know any of it was there. Couldn't I at least just close my eyes?

Eyes Wide Open

No, I guess the eyes-closed way is not always best. Second Kings 6 tells of a time when a warring king had surrounded Elisha's entire city. Verse 15 says that there were troops, horses, and chariots everywhere. They were in a situation a gajillion times stickier than any two-year-old sucker. Elisha's servant asked what in the world they should do, and Elisha replied, "Don't be afraid! For our army is bigger than theirs!" (v. 16 TLB).

I can imagine Elisha's servant fighting the urge to say, "So, Elisha—math is not your thing, huh?" But Elisha did something grand that he really didn't have to do. He asked God to open his servant's eyes. Verse 17 says, "The Lord opened the young man's eyes so that he could see horses of fire and chariots of fire everywhere upon the mountain!" (TLB). A heavenly army that numbered more than the miscellaneous pieces of any VCR!

Believing Is Seeing!

How many times is my faith about as small as my earthly vision? I can all too often become like Thomas who wouldn't believe until he could see for himself. Jesus said to him in John 20:29, "Because you have seen me, you have believed; blessed are those who have not seen and yet have believed."

Seeing is believing. But believing without seeing—that's real faith. It's a truly priceless faith (*priceless*—no price tag needed). Do you ever wonder what the heavenly Father might be doing this very minute that we can't see? Do we trust him in complete faith even when he doesn't "open our eyes" to those things? We're given a good definition of eyes-open/eyes-closed faith in Hebrews 11:1: "Now faith is being sure of what we hope for and certain of what we do not see." Now that's a firm belief. And if I'm a firm believer in full shoe-gluttony disclosure, I'm a firmer believer in this most wondrous kind of disclosure! The firmest.

As we grow in that "believing without seeing" kind of faith, we realize that sometimes sandals are the best kind of high heels for walking in the highest places. Heading for high places with Christ and growing in the knowledge of God as Colossians 1:10 teaches means growing in our faith. It's the kind of faith growth that produces an ever-changing life—the kind of faith that leads us to "follow in Jesus's sandals" with total abandon. Off with the high heels, on with the sandals? Whatever it takes!

It's positively astonishing to stop and think about the way our God works. As we grow in faith, we follow in the footsteps of Jesus more closely; and as we follow in those sandal steps of Jesus more closely, our faith grows. It's an amazing sandal circle of our faith life!

I'm asking God to continue to grow me up in the knowledge of him, with an eyes-wide-open faith, even when my eyes are closed. You can ask him to grow you in God-knowledge and in your faith life too. Watch your faith grow, and you'll watch some of the biggest things happen in this life—bigger than you ever could have imagined.

And speaking of "big imagining," if you can muster even the smallest concept of Kaley's closet, you probably do have a pretty big imagination.

> The fundamental fact of existence is that this trust in God, this faith, is the firm foundation under everything that makes life worth living. It's our handle on what we can't see. The act of faith is what distinguished our ancestors, set them above the crowd. By faith, we see the world called into existence by God's word, what we see created by what we don't see.
>
> *Hebrews 11:1–3 Message*

part 6

"may you be strengthened
with all power, according
to his glorious might"

waiting for the other shoe to drop

21

It really is like waiting for the other shoe to drop.

"I get the front seat!"

I'll bet I've heard that battle cry over a million times. It was usually followed by someone else shouting, "Nuh uh, first one there gets it!" That sounded the charge.

After I heard the charge, I would instinctively cringe as I waited for the other shoe to drop, as it were. Actually, at least one shoe would usually fly first, then drop. It was typically a flip-flop. Have you ever seen a herd of kids in a stampede, and just about all you could make out was a cloud of dust and a few flying flip-flops?

I would always watch incredulously (you'd think I'd have gotten used to it after a million-plus times) as the herd of determined, wild-eyed kids dashed for the coveted passenger seat of the car. A few moos and various other cattle noises, and the stampede scene would've been complete. I would invariably be shouting warnings toward the herd to stop running and watch for cars as they darted through traffic and leaped over potholes. My shouts were pretty futile. The kids never heard them. Every word was tuned out and entirely too late anyway. They didn't hear because they were focused on the goal: *Shotgun.*

The kids never seemed to completely grasp certain laws of thermal dynamics. They didn't slow down. I would watch and wince as they plastered each other against the car door. Another five-kid pileup.

Twenty Seconds FLAT

The passenger seat race would usually take only about twenty seconds, but there was almost always a questionable finish. It was a photo finish with no photo. You'd think it would be easy enough to find the winner. After the other kids are peeled off, it should be the kid who's smashed the flattest against the door. Flattest kid wins, right? But after some loud and animated squabbling from the shoeless pancake kids, I often ended up driving home with the front seat all to myself. I would end the entire episode with one of those Solomon-type motherly moments: "If you're going to run like crazy people through a busy parking lot, and if you're going to argue over something so silly, then I'm going to have to cut the passenger seat in two . . . I mean . . . then you're all in the backseat."

For the duration of the ride, there would be all kinds of death whispers coming from the back. "You know I was first." "You never said 'go.'" "You were standing on my flip-flop." It's amazing how the race could be long over, but the battle still raged on.

Fight the Good Fight

This life is like a battle—a much bigger battle. Ephesians 6:12–13 says,

> For our battle is not against flesh and blood, but against the rulers, against the authorities, against the world powers of this darkness,

against the spiritual forces of evil in the heavens. This is why you must take up the full armor of God, so that you may be able to resist in the evil day, and having prepared everything, to take your stand.

HCSB

There's a spiritual battle raging, and we're instructed to stand—never fall!

Making a stand in this life is not about getting the best seat in the car. It's fighting the "good" fight. Paul said in 2 Timothy 4:7, "I have fought the good fight, I have finished the race, I have kept the faith." The "good" fight is never over the petty things we quibble over in our own flesh. And it's not a battle we fight in our own strength, but one we fight in his strength, with the armor he provides. What a list of battle gear in Ephesians 6:14–17: the belt of truth, the breastplate of righteousness, the gospel of peace, the shield of faith, the helmet of salvation, and the sword of the Spirit, the Word of God. Everything we need to be battle-ready!

Shooting for Shotgun?

In 2 Timothy 4:7, *The Message* describes the good fight as "the only race worth running." The whole passage reminds us to keep our eyes focused on Jesus and his coming. It has a purifying effect in our lives and keeps us fit, ready to run toward every worthy goal. Our focus should be as clear as a passenger-side door to a herd of sprinting kids.

How often do we let other battles steal away our focus? Every now and then I have to take a little battle inventory in my own life. I can't tell you how often I'm surprised to find myself in battles that have nothing to do with the eternal essentials of life. I hate it when I have to yell at myself, "Hey! This is not the 'good' fight." I can so easily end up tripping in a big fat pothole.

We have a scheming enemy who is digging each carefully placed pothole. He would like nothing better than to see us trip in one and fall flat. He would love to render every Christian powerless. But Colossians 1:11 reminds us that we are anything but powerless when we're depending on the Source of all power—the one with all-glorious might!

No need to fear the dark spiritual forces you can't see. Don't fret over the battle. It's God's strength that wins it, not ours. But we should never tune out the warnings to run in the right way and in the right direction. As long as we're running in the right direction, we'll never get flattened. It's like riding shotgun with Jesus.

Fleet of Foot

In God's strength we are sure-footed, whether we're wearing high heels, our running tennies, or even flying flip-flops. It's his strength that will take us to those high places. Habakkuk 3:19 says, "The Sovereign LORD is my strength; he makes my feet like the feet of a deer, he enables me to go on the heights."

The Amplified Bible expands it this way:

The Lord God is my Strength, my personal bravery, and my invincible army; He makes my feet like hinds' feet and will make me to walk [not to stand still in terror, but to walk] and make [spiritual] progress upon my high places [of trouble, suffering, or responsibility]!

Progress on high places in the strength of the Lord God!

Praise God that he is our invincible army! His kind of invincible army is more powerful than any evil forces. More powerful than a locomotive, for that matter. Even more powerful than a herd of stampeding kids!

> Finally, be strong in the Lord and in his mighty power. Put on the full armor of God so that you can take your stand against the devil's schemes. For our struggle is not against flesh and blood, but against the rulers, against the authorities, against the powers of this dark world and against the spiritual forces of evil in the heavenly realms. Therefore put on the full armor of God, so that when the day of evil comes, you may be able to stand your ground, and after you have done everything, to stand. Stand firm then, with the belt of truth buckled around your waist, with the breastplate of righteousness in place, and with your feet fitted with the readiness that comes from the gospel of peace. In addition to all this, take up the shield of faith, with which you can extinguish all the flaming arrows of the evil one. Take the helmet of salvation and the sword of the Spirit, which is the word of God.
>
> *Ephesians 6:10–17*

shoe box faith   22

High heels are such high fun in so many ways. Even the boxes they come in. Oh, the many uses of a shoe box! They store photos, crayons, and love letters. They're incredibly handy for making shadow boxes or dolly beds. Hey, some people have even been known to store shoes in them!

Need more uses for shoe boxes? How about these?

101 Uses for a Shoe Box (Minus 91)

1. It can hold all the ballots from the class monitor election run-off in Mrs. Harris's sixth grade science class (hey, we hang on to those victories that give us the power to write names on the board).
2. A shoe box can store fashion doll bodies and their dolly heads—but not necessarily intact. You usually have to snap off the heads or they won't fit. Looks a little gruesome, but none of them have complained.
3. Without the box, a box lunch would be really tough to carry—and a "pocket lunch" just wouldn't be the same.
4. It makes a really terrible time capsule, but most kids don't realize it until all their treasures for the future have decomposed (who really needed to be reminded of the disco years, anyway?).
5. A shoe box is a pretty good place to store your fleas until you train them for your circus.
6. With enough black crayon, it makes an acceptable hamster casket.
7. It's great for storing all those bread ties that you don't know why you're keeping but just can't bring yourself to throw away.
8. With enough of them, you can play a giant game of shoe box Jenga.
9. They're perfect for storing those eight-track tapes.
10. If you collect a few shoe boxes, you can store lots of superfluous information in them—such as the many uses of shoe boxes.

Kids, of course, can come up with even more uses. To them a shoe box is a cardboard playground. All boxes, for that matter. Amazing, isn't it? You can spend a fortune on the toddler PlayStation to end all toddler PlayStations. It encourages basic reading skills (in English, Spanish, and Portuguese), helps hone fine motor skills, teaches basic chemistry principles, develops social and political awareness, and teaches toddlers how to recognize the subtle nuances of Beethoven. All that and you still find that your toddler gets a much bigger kick out of the big box it came in. Isn't it hilarious that the empty box can mean more to a kid than the budget-breaking gift we were sure he had to have?

Thinking Outside the Box

As strange as it may sound, sometimes the best gift we can give our heavenly Father is our emptiness. Like the box without the extravagant toy. My Kaley may not have the neatest closet and the most organized shoe boxes in town, but when it comes to the bigger, more important box issues, she gets it. I don't know how I could've been more moved when I read the poem she wrote last year called "The Gift." It's a stirring reminder to me that when we present our emptiness to our King, by his eternal, mighty power, he fills us with eternal worth and everything we need to walk the worthy walk.

The Gift

by Kaley Faith Rhea

The innocence of early morning sunlight
Reflects in the eyes of the young child
His eyes, deeper somehow than an uncaring world could
    fathom

His eyes, focused solely on his King

The world, so busy in its preparation, cannot stand still
for a moment
Cannot stand still to marvel at the One for whom they
prepare
His feet, stepping timidly toward the One he so admires
His feet, tip-toeing past the throngs of rushing people

"The King is coming! The King is coming!" Yet still they
cannot see
The Person they long to recognize stands but a few yards
away
His hands, cradling a precious gift, unwrapped and
unadorned
His hands, reach out to tug the sleeve of the One he holds
the highest

But then those hands are pulled away by the people of the
world
Angry faces and scalding glares, "You must work to earn
your way"
His tears, hot and salty, flow down the young boy's face
His tears, each carrying shame and hurt, for he can see
his King no more

A strong hand brings comfort as it rests upon his head
And then the boy is turned into a seldom-felt embrace
His face, dirty and tear-stained, buries itself in a broad
shoulder
His face, feeling the kiss of soft velvet, looks up in shock
and awe

The King looked down at him and smiled, a smile that lit
the sky
And gently asked just what it was the boy was crying for
His words, halting and unsteady, told of the gift he'd
meant to give
His words, full of great respect, made the King's eyes mist
a bit

"Don't mind the others," the King said sadly, "They're
blind to what is real
"Spending time getting themselves ready, they forget to
spend time with Me"
His gift, held out readily, a small, plain, wooden box
His gift, when opened revealed nothing, only emptiness
inside

"If I tried to fill this box," the child explained with care,
"It would have no worth at all
"But if you were to fill it with anything you have, it would
be worth the world and more"
His love, shown by his gift, words, face, tears, hands, feet,
and eyes, brought music to the scene
His love, a joyful melody to the King, the only gift for
which He'd asked[7]

Wow, what a beautiful picture of an all-powerful, all-knowing
King! What do we have to offer? Nothing really. An empty box.
But as we offer our love and our emptiness, he makes something
wonderful from our weakness by his own power and might. He
fills us with himself!

In Ephesians 3:18–20, Paul talks about the high love of God.
We can't fully understand it, but we can be "fully filled" by it.

And may you have the power to understand, as all God's people should, how wide, how long, how high, and how deep his love really is. May you experience the love of Christ, though it is so great you will never fully understand it. Then you will be filled with the fullness of life and power that comes from God. Now glory be to God! By his mighty power at work within us, he is able to accomplish infinitely more than we would ever dare to ask or hope.

NLT

All by his "mighty power at work within us"!

A Big Box of Faith

Our faith is well placed when it rests in the one who has all might and power. Psalm 89:13–15 shouts it: "You are strong and mighty! Your kingdom is ruled by justice and fairness with love and faithfulness leading the way. Our LORD, you bless those who join in the festival and walk in the brightness of your presence" (CEV). His strength and might are infinitely bigger than any "writing names on the board" power. He's taking names in the best way—he has lovingly written them in his Book of Life!

Understanding his strength strengthens our faith—sounds like a lot of muscle all around, doesn't it? He strengthens us with his might because he cares about us and loves us with the deepest, most perfect love. Every ounce of his own might he uses to strengthen us is like a glowing love note.

Now there's something to tuck away in a shoe box!

I ask him to strengthen you by his Spirit—not a brute strength but a glorious inner strength—that Christ will live in you as you open the door and invite him in. And I ask him that with both feet planted firmly on love, you'll be able to take in with all followers of

Jesus the extravagant dimensions of Christ's love. Reach out and experience the breadth! Test its length! Plumb the depths! Rise to the heights! Live full lives, full in the fullness of God.

Ephesians 3:16–19 Message

step up to the gate 23

Let me tell you, I know my shoe shopping. QVC has nothing on me. I can sniff out the best places for the best shoe bargains anywhere in the Midwest. You might say I have a nose for feet.

No need to have special sniffing abilities when it comes to my kids' shoes, though. I always know it's time to get the industrial-strength drum of Febreze out when I come home and realize my entire house smells like kid feet. As I get closer to the boys' rooms, I realize the smell is more like the zoo. The monkey cages at the zoo. That's usually the point I go in with the Febreze, but the Febreze begins to cry. As a matter of fact, somewhere near Daniel's baseball shoes, the Febreze goes into a deep, dark depression, curls up in the fetal position in the corner, rocking back and forth, mumbling something about rethinking its purpose in life.

I've come up with a simple solution to the problem of the baseball shoe stench: baseball sandals. They could air themselves out as the game went along. Brilliant, isn't it?

De Agony of De Cleats

I was ready to put on a hazmat suit, get a chain saw, and cut the toes and heels out of Daniel's cleats, but he had some serious objections. According to him, you have to be careful what kind of shoes you play ball in. He seemed to think sandals could leave a little too much room for serious toe damage. He had a point.

At least the sandal cleats wouldn't be as dangerous as high heels. Not that Daniel has ever asked to play ball in high heels, incidentally. He wanted me to be sure to mention that part. I told him the high heel cleats topic fits because it's a book about high heels, not because he wears them. I think that disclaimer prevents this chapter of the book from challenging his young manhood.

High heels are fine for high places, but for baseball? High heels are definitely out. Don't even need the three strikes—they're out. While a girls' team would look absolutely adorable in high heel cleats, I can't imagine what kind of holes they could poke in the bases. And sliding? That could put an eye out.

Manly Daniel tells me that baseball is a sport for the rough and tough, anyway. You have to be ready and willing to step up to the plate, as it were.

Just for the record, even the manly Daniel wasn't exactly Mr. Rough and Tough several months ago at the doctor's office. The twelve-year-old manly man had to have a finger prick. Don't you hate those?

Sticking It to the Man

I wasn't exactly rough and tumble myself. I felt so badly for him, poor thing. He told me later he thought the needle was going to come all the way through the other side of his finger.

He got really nervous when the nurse couldn't seem to get enough blood from the first stick. We were all thinking she might have to go after another finger. But that determined nurse knew he hated the idea of skewering another finger, and she kept squeezing that first one for all it was worth. Daniel kept smiling, but it was a smile with a wince. She all but had him in a headlock. She finally managed to wring out enough for his blood test. Whew!

I told Daniel during the finger milking that we could drive through the fast-food restaurant of his choice once we wrapped up the doctor's office visit. After all, every kid who has to have a finger prick deserves a mercy burger, right?

After the nurse left the room, I asked him where he'd like to go for lunch. He said, "I haven't had a chance to think about it yet. I was too busy trying to bleed."

Out of Control

He's so funny.

We all get a little funny on the spiritual side too. We try to control things that are totally out of our power to control. It's about as futile as trying to bleed.

There's only one who truly controls everything. In Ephesians 1:19–22, Paul prays that we'll understand the oh-so-mighty, death-conquering power of the all-controlling one.

I pray that you will begin to understand the incredible greatness of his power for us who believe him. This is the same mighty power that raised Christ from the dead and seated him in the place of honor at God's right hand in the heavenly realms. Now he is far above any ruler or authority or power or leader or anything else in this world or in the world to come. And God has put all things under the authority of Christ, and he gave him this authority for the benefit of the church.

NLT

All the control in the universe is safely where it should be—in Christ. Paul tells us it's for our benefit. It really is good for us when we understand that he is in control and when we quit trying to run things on our own.

Praise the Lord who so mightily controls the stars and planets, land and seas—our very hearts and each heart's every beat. That does include, by the way, every drop of blood those hearts are pumping—from every ventricle to every finger and back.

God controls our here and he controls our now. He controls our future too. And that's a good thing. When we understand that the almighty God controls it all, not only do we step up to the plate to go higher places, but we get a glimpse of a marvelous future. We will someday step up to the gates—the pearly ones. "No mere man has ever seen, heard or even imagined what wonderful things God has ready for those who love the Lord" (1 Cor. 2:9 TLB).

Here, now, always, and forever. What a mighty God we serve!

What a God we have! And how fortunate we are to have him, this Father of our Master Jesus! Because Jesus was raised from the dead, we've been given a brand-new life and have everything to live for, including a future in heaven—and the future starts now! God is keeping careful watch over us and the future. The Day is coming when you'll have it all—life healed and whole.

1 Peter 1:3–5 Message

24   you put your right foot in

Have you ever noticed what the right pair of shoes can do for your mood? You slide your feet into just the right pair and a bit of a transformation happens. Amazing, isn't it? Suddenly you don't feel quite as tired. The corners of your mouth just might begin to turn upward in at least a semi-perky little grin. The right shoes are a little like mood batteries. Talk about a pick-me-up. Newfound energy right there at your toe-tips! No wait, better than batteries. The right shoes are like chocolate for your feet!

While We're Covering Chocolate

Speaking of chocolate, like 97 percent of the over-civilized world, I start a new diet just about every January 1. The good news is that I think I've finally hit on a diet I can stick with. It's an all-salad diet. Any and every salad is considered health food, right? So why not a hot-fudge-topped chocolate chip and spinach salad? Hide a pork chop and gravy in there and you can hit every corner of the food pyramid (and hit those corners hard). And you should see my Ding Dong salad. It's a beautiful thing. Slice a couple of those chocolate beauties over a bed of iceberg and you've got yourself some health food you can sink your teeth into. Mmm, I love salad.

It inspired my own "Salad Song"—destined to be a classic:

> Chocolate, chocolate can't be beat
> Chocolate dark or semi-sweet
> Chocolate cakes and chocolate candy
> Blood sugar's up but I'm choco-dandy
>
> Chocolate hot and chocolate cold
> Chocolate new and vintage old
> Chocolate makes a lovely ballad
> And the perfect topping for my health food salad

Just as chocolate can transform even an all-salad diet into something sweet, we let God transform our lives into something sweet when we allow him to change our thinking. We looked at Romans 12:1–2 earlier. Take a look in another translation:

> Dear friends, God is good. So I beg you to offer your bodies to him as a living sacrifice, pure and pleasing. That's the most sensible way to serve God. Don't be like the people of this world, but let God change the way you think. Then you will know how to do everything that is good and pleasing to him.
>
> CEV

That means I need to put my brain on the altar. Not necessarily a pleasant visual, but it really is a good way to live. It's the worthy walk. And that worthy walk is not just a lifestyle choice. It's a calling.

Paul said in Ephesians 4:1–3, "I, therefore, the prisoner of the Lord, beseech you to walk worthy of the calling with which you were called, with all lowliness and gentleness, with longsuffering, bearing with one another in love, endeavoring to keep the unity of the Spirit in the bond of peace" (NKJV).

The calling affects every direction we choose in life and every response to every person and every situation—whether we put our right foot in, our left foot out. No matter which foot goes where, that's how we put our best foot forward. By allowing the calling to the worthy walk to become our center. And whatever the Hokey Pokey says, we don't even necessarily have to shake it all about.

Any time, however, you find yourself walking in a self-focused direction, you can fulfill your calling in Hokey Pokey form—you turn yourself around. Walking worthy. THAT'S what it's all about.

Calling All Worthy Walkers

First Thessalonians 2:11–12 says, "As you know, like a father with his own children, we encouraged, comforted, and implored each one of you to walk worthy of God, who calls you into His own kingdom and glory" (HCSB).

You were called into this walk. With the call comes his power. As a matter of fact, with every calling he gives, God always gives the empowering. He would never call you to a worthy walk if he didn't intend to give you the strength to walk it. Paul makes it plain in Philippians 2:13: "[Not in your own strength] for it is God Who is all the while effectually at work in you [energizing and creating in you the power and desire], both to will and to work for His good pleasure and satisfaction and delight" (AMP). His strength!

If we can learn to believe, trust in, rest in the knowledge that he is all-powerful and that it's his strength that fulfills every calling, we will experience the most pleasurable growth. We'll find ourselves on blessed higher ground with him. A worthy walk is a walk full to overflowing with knowing and trusting him.

We'll never be able to do the will of God without completely trusting in the power of God to do it. When we do trust him to make it happen, we find that he is more than worthy of that trust. First Thessalonians 5:23–24 says, "May God himself, the God of peace, sanctify you through and through. May your whole spirit, soul and body be kept blameless at the coming of our Lord Jesus Christ. The one who calls you is faithful and he will do it."

He calls. He is faithful. What more do we need to know? It's that knowledge that leads us to place our brains on the altar of God—along with every other body part and every spiritual heart part too.

Other Walk Talk

I should mention (in matters of less importance) that since we're giving all our body parts to God, and since we probably don't want to add unnecessary weight to the altar, figuratively speaking, we might want to rethink my salad diet. It's weird, but I've gained eight pounds eating all salads!

> Sing to God, you kingdoms of the earth.
>> Sing praises to the Lord.
> Sing to the one who rides across the ancient heavens,
>> his mighty voice thundering from the sky.
> Tell everyone about God's power.
>> His majesty shines down on Israel;
>> his strength is mighty in the heavens.
> God is awesome in his sanctuary.
>> The God of Israel gives power and strength to his people.
> Praise be to God!

Psalm 68:32–35 NLT

part 7

"for all endurance
and patience"

check the bottom of your shoe

25

How many times has it happened? You see a classy gal exiting the ladies' room, making her grand reentrance to the fancy event. She's a picture of style—and it looks as though she's been practicing. She's been practicing the walk of flair in the highest pumps. No doubt she's also been practicing that cool look—the one that says, "I don't trouble myself with trivial details." Total panache. You wonder if she senses the eyes of everyone in the room snapping to attention—the spotlight is on her.

But about then, she starts to realize that, while she should be hearing oohs and aahs, she's hearing snickers and giggles instead. That's when she looks down to find the twelve-foot toilet paper streamer waving like a nerd flag from her designer high heels.

Do you know how a fluttering TP flag kills an elegant reentrance? Of all the flags to be waving!

Of course, I guess there are worse things to find stuck to the bottom of your shoe. Let's give that topic a little thought.

Top Ten Things You Don't Want to Find Stuck to the Bottom of Your Shoe

10. Plastic explosives and a timer.
9. The nanite prototype you've been working on for twenty years. (Don't you hate it when you squish your micro-robots?)
8. Any body part still attached to your person (this one is mostly for those of us over forty).
7. Your contact lens.
6. The head of a two-inch nail.
5. A twenty-pound chunk of concrete (which is especially problematic if you find yourself at the bottom of a river).
4. An oozing tube of something glowing, marked "Danger! Toxic Material."
3. A small piece of your paycheck.
2. The side of a building—especially if you've recently been bitten by a radioactive spider and web-goo keeps shooting out of your wrists.
1. Lilliputians.

I have friends who are much too organized to ever find anything stuck to their shoes that doesn't belong. Nothing is ever out of place long enough to get stepped on. I have a friend who has a special loofah for each day of the week and hangs them in order, who has never left a dirty dish sitting in the sink for more than fifteen minutes. Her shoes are organized in her closet by size, shape, color, outfit, height of heel, and season—maybe price too.

I love having those kinds of friends. I borrow things from them a lot—because they can actually find stuff. I love them, often wish I *was* them, but sadly, there are hardly any similarities. I have a few pockets of organization in my life. Well, probably just enough to keep my family from going completely insane and to keep my editors from losing their spirituality. But much of my life is spent hunting through large piles of junk I should have thrown away, searching for the life-or-death kind of important items I've misplaced.

Trash Pickup?

I do have one friend, however, who is much more like me than I'm sure she would ever want anyone to know. Organization? Not exactly her watchword either. Her pickup, for instance, looks like it belongs to a homeless person. You would almost swear all her worldly goods are in there.

I took a ride in her truck recently, and I actually had to sit on a two-foot pile of junk mail, candy wrappers, books, file folders, and takeout bags from at least a couple of month s' worth of fast food. There had to have been six pairs of shoes on the floorboard (I had to respect that). They were sitting on top of a pile of clothes. I think she could've been locked out of her house for a solid week without experiencing any real wardrobe shortages.

I started to sit down on her taxes and noticed there was enough Bible study material under there to cause significant face glowage à la Moses. But all fashion, government, and spiritual stuff aside, I had to draw the line at sitting on the can of biscuits I saw poking out from under some Styrofoam containers.

"Hey, I'm not sitting on a can of biscuits. What if it pops open and explodes biscuit shrapnel all over my rear end?" It's one thing to have to scrape goo off my shoe, but off my backside?

"No way," she laughed. "It's been in here since last Christmas. Even if it popped open, the insides are probably too shriveled to do any damage." She still humored me and tossed the thing on the dashboard.

I wasn't convinced that the shriveled goo wouldn't morph. Had she never seen the movie *The Blob*?

I stared at the blobette as it rolled back and forth on the dash. "You have to know that could put an eye out." Even as I said it, I pictured an entire office of health insurance personnel puzzled over where to file a claim reading "Cause of injury: accidentally assailed by canned bread product." You really have to be careful what you stare at. And you really have to be careful what you sit on.

What Am I Sitting On?

Funny that I should worry about what I was sitting on when worry itself can be such a dangerous thing to sit on. Jesus knew we would have worrying tendencies. He addressed it point blank in Matthew 6:27 when he asked, "Who of you by worrying can add a single hour to his life?"

Every now and then, we need to do a little self-exam. We need to ask ourselves if there's anything we're sitting on that we shouldn't be. Are there any worries threatening to explode worry-goo all over our lives? Not only is it not adding a single hour to life, it can actually suck some of the goodness out of life.

Philippians 4:6–7 tells us what to do instead of worrying:

Don't fret or worry. Instead of worrying, pray. Let petitions and praises shape your worries into prayers, letting God know your concerns. Before you know it, a sense of God's wholeness, everything coming together for good, will come and settle you down. It's wonderful what happens when Christ displaces worry at the center of your life.

Message

Living a fretful life is no way to live. It's the way to get ulcers. When we're worried, we're consumed by whatever it is we're fretting over—even if it's something that hasn't happened. The focus of our worry becomes all we can think about. That means we're not able to focus where we really need to. How can our focus be on worry and on Christ at the same time? It's the opposite of the "endurance with patience" Colossians 1:11 speaks of. Endurance means not getting distracted. How many of us get so distracted by worry that we can't focus on the purpose God has for us? No patience. No joy. Just worry.

We can trade worry for prayer and for a purpose focus. It's a trade that brings the peace of God. If you're struggling with anxiety, ask God to give you his peace. Through prayer, trade worry for his presence and his purpose, and then you'll be better able to get going in working for him.

De-doughing

Incidentally, it might be one less thing for you to worry about if I go ahead and tell you that there were no bread-related injuries reported after the truck ride. No dough-covered booty. What a relief. I might've had to ask my organized friend if I could borrow her loofahs. Hey, for that kind of cleanup, her scrubbies could've been gummed up from Tuesday clear through Saturday!

> Therefore I tell you, stop being perpetually uneasy (anxious and worried) about your life, what you shall eat or what you shall drink; or about your body, what you shall put on. Is not life greater [in quality] than food, and the body [far above and more excellent] than clothing? Look at the birds of the air; they neither sow nor reap nor gather into barns, and yet your heavenly Father keeps feeding

them. Are you not worth much more than they? And who of you by worrying and being anxious can add one unit of measure (cubit) to his stature or to the span of his life? . . . Therefore do not worry and be anxious, saying, What are we going to have to eat? Or, What are we going to have to drink? Or, What are we going to have to wear? For the Gentiles (heathen) wish for and crave and diligently seek all these things, and your heavenly Father knows well that you need them all. But seek (aim at and strive after) first of all His kingdom and His righteousness (His way of doing and being right), and then all these things taken together will be given you besides.

Matthew 6:25–27, 31–33 AMP

26 shoes that work in a pinch

I found the perfect shoes to go with my taupe suit. Perfect, I tell you. They're just the right shade of that unidentifiable tan/gray (you know, the color that women won't admit they can't identify and all men call "brown"). They have the pointiest toe—the kind that's supposed to make my feet look like model feet, even though I'm a foot too short and another foot too wide. I'm telling you, these shoes are so wonderfully pointy, I think I could climb telephone poles in these alligator beauties. Oh they're not real alligator, but still just the right fake gator pattern to go with that suit. As soon as I saw the faux alligators, I knew I had to snap them up.

To top it all off (in the highest heel heights), the heels on these shoes make me look three and a half inches taller than I really am. That's an important three and a half inches when you've got the foot-too-short, foot-too-wide thing going. A well-placed faux alligator on the right foot can be a thing of beauty.

Foot-Folding

The only problem with the perfect pair of shoes is that I have to fold my feet in several different spots to squish them into these puppies. It's like foot origami. I can wear them for about twenty minutes. Then I'm dying. Oh, the things we'll do to look great for twenty minutes.

I wore the shoes to a big event recently. They looked great . . . dangling from my *wrist*. I'm trying to convince my husband they were a real bargain because I can wear them as heels or as lovely and very versatile bracelets. He's not buying it. In more ways than one.

He all but asked me to take them back when the debit charge went through and we heard that sucking sound coming from our bank account. I won't tell you what they cost, but let's just say I was afraid my hubby was going to require a little CPR. How am I going to tell him I need an alligator purse to match? Clear!

Charging On in a Pinch

Poor Richie. He should be at least a little used to it by now. After all, I have that whole debit thing down to an art. I can eyeball a great pair of shoes, swoop them off the store shelf, and swipe my debit card all in one smooth movement. I'm pretty sure I've got it honed down to about a two-second swoop and swipe. Art in motion.

But while I call it an "art," my husband may very well have another name for it. Oh well, you know what they say. "One person's art is another person's myocardial infarction." It's all in how you look at things.

Wouldn't it be nice if this life didn't require any of that "endurance and patience" Paul mentions in Colossians 1:11? Wouldn't it be great if cute shoes never pinched? But that's just not the way it is this side of heaven. In a world affected by sin, there are going to be troubles—pinches of all kinds.

Refining Steps

When times are tough and shoes are the tightest, we can see a difficult setback as a crushing defeat and the absence of God working, or we can see it as part of a refining process he wants to use in our lives to conform us to the image of Christ. First Peter 4:12–13 says, "Friends, when life gets really difficult, don't jump to the conclusion that God isn't on the job. Instead, be glad that you are in the very thick of what Christ experienced. This is a spiritual refining process, with glory just around the corner" (Message).

Are you in a struggle, wondering where God is in the midst of your pain? Are you wondering how you missed the will of God? Here's something important to note when you're in a pinch. Sometimes you can be in the midst of a humongous struggle and still be right in the center of God's will. He can use struggles and pain in our lives to remind us that this life isn't all there is. He can even use those very struggles to refine us into more of the women of God he wants us to be.

In Mark 4:37–40 we're told about a struggle the disciples experienced:

> And a great windstorm arose, and the waves beat into the boat, so that it was already filling. But He was in the stern, asleep on a pillow. And they awoke Him and said to Him, "Teacher, do You not care that we are perishing?" Then He arose and rebuked the wind, and said to the sea, "Peace, be still!" And the wind ceased and there was a great calm. But He said to them, "Why are you so fearful? How is it that you have no faith?"
>
> NKJV

Where's Jesus?

The disciples were experiencing a huge struggle—a giant storm. Where was Jesus in the midst of their struggle? *He was right there with them.* Yep, he was in the boat! Sometimes we can get our focus on the storm and completely miss his presence. To miss his presence is to miss his "Peace, be still" kind of calm assurance.

And let's think it through. Who told the disciples to get in that boat in the first place? It was Jesus, right? So were the disciples in the will of God? Yes!

He could've told the disciples not to get in the boat. God could've kept Daniel out of the lions' den. He could've kept Shadrach, Meshach, and Abednego out of that fiery furnace. But he didn't. And because he didn't, each of them has a name recorded in the pages of the Holy Bible. Their names and their stories have been proclaiming the sufficiency of God for every pinch in every life for thousands of years. Each one of them came out of the struggles stronger in faith.

Power Struggles

Our struggles cause us to look to the Lord and to depend on him for strength instead of trying to rely on ourselves. Sometimes in a struggle, he can show his power like nowhere else. Not necessarily by making the storm go away, but by miraculously working in the life of his beloved child. By bringing her peace in the midst of the storm. He is more powerful than any storm you're facing. If you're in a storm, let the pinch teach you to trust him. There's no need to fear when he is with you.

Jesus asked his disciples after he calmed the storm, "Why are you so fearful? How is it that you have no faith?" That had to be a little embarrassing. Hello. Disciples. Creator of the universe right there in the boat with you. What are you whining about?

No Fear

We need to recognize God's presence and let it bolster our faith when we hit struggles. Psalm 23 is one of the best-loved, most widely read, quoted, and memorized chapters in the Bible. "Yea, though I walk through the valley of the shadow of death, I will fear no evil." Why doesn't the psalmist fear? Verse 4 says, "For you are with me." He is with you in the valley. He's with you in the boat. In the furnace, in the lions' den—in every big pinch and every small one. He is with you.

If you're in the midst of an overwhelming "refining process" right now, hang on. There's hope—hope of glory just around the corner. Second Corinthians 4:17 tells us that "our light and momentary troubles are achieving for us an eternal glory that far outweighs them all." Let your troubles inspire you to become more like Jesus, who suffered with great grace. Let them refine you. Let them deepen your faith and courage.

Meanwhile, Back on the Shallow Side . . .

Regarding those not-so-deep issues, I'm encouraging Richie to have courage too. He'll need it. I'm going shopping for that purse. Gator hunting!

If he cries, would those be considered alligator tears?

You, Lord, are my shepherd. I will never be in need. You let me rest in fields of green grass. You lead me to streams of peaceful water, and you refresh my life. You are true to your name, and you lead me along the right paths. I may walk through valleys as dark as death, but I won't be afraid. You are with me, and your shepherd's rod makes me feel safe. You treat me to a feast, while my enemies watch. You honor me as your guest, and you fill my cup until it overflows. Your kindness and love will always be with me each day of my life, and I will live forever in your house, LORD.

Psalm 23 CEV

---

stepping-stones can break your bones

27

Whenever we hit a rocky place in life, isn't it almost required that we immediately trot our high heels right over to hit the ice cream shop for a dip or two? I think the ice cream engineers invented "Rocky Road" for such a time as this.

There seems to be great therapy in a frozen chocolate treat. Oh yes, it's got to be ice cream. Don't try a hunk of beef jerky—Slim Jims won't do it for you when life gets tough. A cob of corn? Puh-lease. Like any real source of vitamins and minerals will help you. No, you need subzero, sugar-laden dairy with some significant chocolate.

The Inside Scoop on Ice Cream

There's something medicinal in just about every one of those thirty-one flavors. You're not likely to hear it at the doctor's office, but personally, I love the sweet Rx to "take two dips and call me in the morning." The double-dipper is a good way to double your pleasure—in a clone-cone sort of way. Then again, cone, cup, sundae, malt, or shake—I never met a chocolate ice cream dessert I didn't like.

Sadly, too many double dips and we can suddenly look down to find we have double the hips too. If the frozen-treat syndrome becomes a habit we can't "shake," does that make it something more like *vice* cream?

Still, most of us feel it's okay to have a taste or two of medicinal ice cream when we're going through trials. Maybe it's one of my shallower intuits, but I can easily picture heading to higher places, tightly holding the Father's hand with one hand and grasping a double-dip cone with sprinkles in the other.

Vice or not, on the rockiest of roads, sometimes we just have to scream for ice cream. Then again, sometimes we just want to scream.

In the last chapter, we touched on the Twenty-third Psalm and its assurance that Jesus is there with us in those rocky valleys. We can even let the rocks on that rocky road become stepping-stones to higher places with the Father. That's patient endurance. Sometimes those stepping-stones might be a little jagged and painful, but if we keep on stepping, we find they really are the way through the rough places.

There are times we need to exercise a little extra patience in that valley too. James 1:2–4 says,

> Consider it a sheer gift, friends, when tests and challenges come at you from all sides. You know that under pressure, your faith-life is forced into the open and shows its true colors. So don't try to get out of anything prematurely. Let it do its work so you become mature and well-developed, not deficient in any way.
>
> Message

Sprint the Rocky Road?

We can get a little too anxious to get out of our troubles no matter what it takes, instead of allowing them to accomplish their maturing work in us. We may miss some big things God wants to do in our lives when we do that. Have you ever noticed that it says in Psalm 23:4, "Yea, though I *walk* through the valley"? It doesn't say, "Yea, though I *hurry* through the valley." It's not "Yea, though I *sprint*" either. I don't see any running there (like we could run in these heels anyway).

Sometimes we need to take the rocks as they come and let the Lord do his complete work in our lives, making us more complete in him, leaning on him every step of the way, remembering his "for thou art with me" presence. Those are the very rocks that can become stepping-stones to higher places. And these stepping-stones won't really break our bones. They can actually build strength— persevering, patiently enduring strength.

We have a lot to do with whether those rocks become stepping-stones or not. We get to decide if we're going to hold his hand through our struggles, like a little child reaching up to grab on to her daddy, or if we're going to jut out our lip and become angry and bitter. We choose. And choosing well is one of the secrets to enduring with joy.

Ice Cream or No, You Can Lick This

How do you endure patiently and joyfully when circumstances are anything but sweet and creamy? You can do it. You can lick fear, worry, and all the rest when you hang on to that hope that your troubles are not going to last forever. Pain seems long and burdensome when we're in the middle of it, but there's unfathomable joy in our future. "Weeping may endure for a night, but joy comes in the morning" (Ps. 30:5 NKJV).

Here's endurance in a nutshell: "Keep your eyes on Jesus, our leader and instructor. He was willing to die a shameful death on the cross because of the joy he knew would be his afterwards" (Heb.12:2 TLB). Eyes on Jesus, eyes on the joy ahead, following Christ's example. And the joy isn't temporary like the struggle and pain. The joy is eternal. There's just no comparison between the temporary struggle and the everlasting joy.

Healing in Every Broken Place

Remember—know, understand, believe that your heavenly Father will give you everything you need to make it through the rocky valley. Remember that he is your rescuer. Psalm 34:18 says, "The LORD is close to the brokenhearted; he rescues those who are crushed in spirit" (NLT). Are you brokenhearted? Does your crushed spirit need to be rescued? Let your Father do the most glorious rescue work in your heart. Let him come close and heal your heart's broken places. His healing reaches deeper than your deepest hurt—and he wants you to have real and lasting joy and to be spiritually whole and eternally healed.

Have you been hunting for strength and joy in your rocky circumstances and wondering why you're not finding it? The last part of verse 11 in Colossians 1 includes the vital tag "with joy." It's time to let the bigger picture become your focus and let Jesus become your joy and your strength. Psalm 84:5–7 reminds us that even when walking through troubles, God gives blessings when we find our strength in him. He really does want you to be strong and joyful. Your strength and joy are beautiful to him!

As a matter of fact, those are the things that will doubly delight our God in the prettiest, most pleasing way. Wouldn't that be a "pretty please"? Maybe we could even say, "Pretty please with sprinkles on top"!

Blessed (happy, fortunate, to be envied) is the man whose strength is in You, in whose heart are the highways to Zion.

Passing through the Valley of Weeping (Baca), they make it a place of springs; the early rain also fills [the pools] with blessings.

They go from strength to strength [increasing in victorious power]; each of them appears before God in Zion.

O Lord God of hosts, hear my prayer; give ear, O God of Jacob! Selah [pause, and calmly think of that]!

Behold our shield [the king as Your agent], O God, and look upon the face of Your anointed!

For a day in Your courts is better than a thousand [anywhere else]; I would rather be a doorkeeper and stand at the threshold in the house of my God than to dwell [at ease] in the tents of wickedness.

For the Lord God is a Sun and Shield; the Lord bestows [present] grace and favor and [future] glory (honor, splendor, and heavenly bliss)! No good thing will He withhold from those who walk uprightly.

O Lord of hosts, blessed (happy, fortunate, to be envied) is the man who trusts in You [leaning and believing on You, committing all and confidently looking to You, and that without fear or misgiving]!

Psalm 84:5–12 AMP

28 take a stroll with your mat

I wonder if my kids' shoes sometimes take little strolls on their own. It's actually a little creepy. I go into one of the kids' rooms, and I catch sight of a pair of shoes just two or three feet from the closet door. Now there's no way my kids would've been that close to where they were supposed to put their shoes away, and then simply have left them right out there where they obviously don't belong and where people could easily trip over them. My kids would never leave such a hazard out there like that.

No, I think the shoes were sneaking out of the closet on their own when I caught them mid-stroll. They always freeze in place, so I've never actually seen them move. They had to be walking out—it's the only explanation.

I don't understand why they don't like staying in the closet. It's a perfect home designed just for shoes and the clothes that go with them. You'd think they'd like having their own place. But they seem to have that wanderlust—itchy feet, you might say. The ins and outs of shoes are very hard to figure.

Coming Out of the Closet, As It Were

As bad as the shoes are about coming out of the closet, I must say the towels are probably much worse about hanging out on their bars. This is a serious matter, especially for a devoted member of the "innie" society. It's not about the ins and outs of society, and it's not a belly-button-related matter. It's a towel-drying issue. I dry off inside the shower, saving my drips and splatters for the drain. My kids, however, are all very ingrained in the outie life.

They get out of the shower, drip all over the floor, dry off, then cover the floor drips with their sopping towels. I've tried to induct them into the innie life, but they can't seem to remember the plan from one shower to the next.

The reason I'm a dedicated innie is that I just hate it when body drippings are slopped all around the bathroom, then left fermenting on the floor in our own personal towel compost. I can't tell you how many times I've checked the bathrooms after a few showers to find that some rogue outie has splattered a trail from shower to sink and beyond. I could probably track down the outies by tracing the slosh, but one slip on the outie trail and I'm afraid I could take a spill myself that would be anything but pleasant to mop up.

There are times I'd totally dismiss the pursuit of determining the innies and outies among my children—if only I could get them to hang up their wet towels. We have innies and outies, yes. But we also have hangers and pilers. The ins and outs of closets and showers—those are complex matters.

Ins and Outs of Conversation

There are ins and outs in conversation too. There are words we're supposed to keep in—innies. Proverbs 17:27–28 says, "A man of knowledge uses words with restraint, and a man of understanding is even-tempered. Even a fool is thought wise if he keeps silent, and discerning if he holds his tongue."

I'm not sure why we don't naturally develop the innie conversation life more. It's a lot like those shoes that have a special space designated for them but choose to walk away from it anyway. Our Master Designer wants our responses to others to be wrapped in loving patience. It's the special, blessed way he's designated for us to live. Why do we so often choose to walk outside that special space? Not only are we outside where we belong, but we so often end up tripping someone else.

How often do we react with inappropriate anger instead of responding with the enduring patience Jesus wants us to have? Anger is the opposite of patience. It's astounding how easily we can shove the patience aside and respond in anger when a difficult person comes along. And by the way, if you don't know any difficult people, then there just aren't all that many people in your life. But showing patience is showing love. In 1 Corinthians 13, the love chapter, Paul leads the list of expressions of love with patience. It's numero uno.

It's interesting that the Greek word for *patience* here means "taking a long time to boil." If we want to walk in high places with God our Father, we need to watch our temperature. I have to ask myself if I'm too often already at a simmer. Do I boil over at the least provocation? Or is love keeping my patience high and my pot cool? Loving patience is quick to listen, quick to forgive, slow to boil.

Designated Outies

On the other hand, there are matters of conversation we're not meant to keep in. Words that are helpful, affirming, beneficial, and kind are clearly meant to be conversation outies. Ephesians 4:29 says, "Do not let any unwholesome talk come out of your mouths, but only what is helpful for building others up according to their needs, that it may benefit those who listen."

Unfortunately, we tend to get the ins and outs of conversation all turned around. We let selfishness tumble right out of our heads and through our mouths, hurting the people we're supposed to be building up. Then we're silent when there's an opportunity to show love and to encourage. But Ephesians 4:2 gives us the instruction to "be completely humble and gentle; be patient, bearing with one another in love." Being patient is a big part of what it means to love.

Take a look at Paul's instructions in 2 Timothy 2:23–24:

> Again I say, don't get involved in foolish, ignorant arguments that only start fights. The Lord's servants must not quarrel but must be kind to everyone. They must be able to teach effectively and be patient with difficult people.
>
> NLT

Our natural response when dealing with difficult people is to become impatient or angry. But Proverbs 19:11 tells us that "a man's wisdom gives him patience; it is his glory to overlook an offense."

Where Do We Hang the Impatience and Anger?

Trying to deal with impatience and anger in our own strength is more futile than trying to get the piler kids to hang their wet towels. We have to come to the place where we thoroughly understand our helplessness without Jesus. It requires a healing, and Jesus is the only one who can heal.

Do you need his healing? In John 5 we're told about a man who had been completely disabled for thirty-eight years. He sat day after day beside a pool that was supposed to have healing powers, knowing that even if the water was stirred with the healing power, he had no way to get to it. The question Jesus asks him is an interesting one: "Do you want to get well?" (v. 6). Thirty-eight years of frustrating infirmity and Jesus asks him if he wants to get well?

I wonder how often we stay stuck in an unfriendly, impatient, unkind, or angry state that we brush off as "just part of our personality." Or with the justification, "It's the way I was brought up—there's no changing now." Or even, "I'm simply genetically wired this way." We even start to depend on that faithful status quo. It doesn't require anything from us to stay stuck in our weakness.

But Christ changes everything. He gives us our own instructions to "Get up! Pick up your mat and walk" (v. 8).

Going to the Mat to Go Higher Places

When Jesus told the man to pick up his mat and walk, he was telling him to pick up what he had been resting on and to take a new direction by faith. It was a place he had never gone before. After spending year after year on that mat on the ground, he was called to go higher places.

We looked at God's nearness to the brokenhearted. Maybe you have allowed him to come near to you to heal some of your broken places. He can heal your angry, bitter places too. Is it time to pick up your mat and walk? Getting up is vital—understanding that God has already done whatever is required. What if Jesus healed the man at the pool of Bethesda but the man didn't believe it had happened? What if he never got up? Imagine finding that long-sought healing, yet staying seated right where he was, crippled and missing out—when, instead, he could be swinging that mat around in the happiest dance.

I'm so convinced that Jesus wants you up and walking away from those areas of bitterness or unkindness that I will guarantee you that if you will let him, he will heal you. Do you want to get well? Your Father doesn't have to change your situation for you to see wellness. He changes you. The Holy Spirit is working in you, and he wants to make those changes happen!

Hang On to This!

When you're dealing with a difficult person and you "don't feel the love," by faith ask the Holy Spirit to love through you. Love is his number one fruit. Don't worry about the ooey-gooey feelings. Feelings follow your faithful obedience. Trust in what Jesus says, get up, and take that mat for a stroll. He said in John 13:34, "A new command I give you: Love one another. As I have loved you, so you must love one another."

Trust his love, trust him, trust his Word—he'll make it happen. We truly can hang on his every word. Hey, doesn't that make us the best kind of hangers?

Now there is in Jerusalem near the Sheep Gate a pool, which in Aramaic is called Bethesda and which is surrounded by five covered colonnades. Here a great number of disabled people used to lie—the blind, the lame, the paralyzed. One who was there had been an invalid for thirty-eight years. When Jesus saw him lying there and learned that he had been in this condition for a long time, he asked him, "Do you want to get well?"

"Sir," the invalid replied, "I have no one to help me into the pool when the water is stirred. While I am trying to get in, someone else goes down ahead of me."

Then Jesus said to him, "Get up! Pick up your mat and walk." At once the man was cured; he picked up his mat and walked.

John 5:2–9

part 8

"with joy giving thanks
to the Father"

these boots are made for thanking 29

Writing thank-you notes can sometimes be more painful than standing all evening at a boring party in four-inch stiletto boots—especially if it's a teenage boy doing the thanking (though I certainly hope we never see any of our teenage boys in four-inch stiletto boots). My son Jordan graduated from high school this year. He got some great gifts (his favorite part of graduating). But how many times did I have to remind him to write those thank-you notes? I was getting a little worried that I might have to physically put the pen in his hand and force it along, word by word.

He finally asked, "Mom, couldn't I just print up a generic thank-you with blanks in it, then fill in the blanks and send 'em?" I smiled and said, "Sure you could, son. If you were FIVE."

Granted, most teenage boys aren't heavily into manners in general. Just the day before, Jordan came upstairs with a look on his face that said he had something significant to announce. He made some exaggerated opera-type motions with his arms, then (with really great posture, I might add) he burp-yelled the words, "I HAVE THE POW-ER!" No kidding. One solid burp.

What a Gas!

I tried not to laugh, really I did. But one solid sentence burp of sonic boom volume? It was just too funny. We all must've laughed for five minutes. Then I wiped my laugh-tears, told him it was NOT funny (still unable to control a few giggle bursts throughout my motherly address) and that he should have better manners than that. The Mom Handbook requires me to make those kinds of disclaimers. That way none of the blame for any manner deficiencies in my kids comes back on me. Of course, after I took care of the disclaimer, I laughed with the rest of the family for another five minutes. At least he did ask to be excused. That was something, right? Yeah, I think that means it was practically an accident.

Sixteen-year-old daughters can come up with good comebacks in these kinds of situations, by the way. After wiping her own laugh-til-she-cried tears, Kaley said, "And you don't have a girlfriend right now?"

I said, "He could if he wanted to. It's not like he doesn't have the POW-ER."

More laughter.

Don't tell my kids, but if I could have burped the last part, I think I would have. Sadly, I just don't have the power.

Missed Manners

Excuse mes and thank-yous are good manners. Jordan may have missed a few etiquette points with the burp-quake, but maybe he made up a few points with his "excuse me." And it took awhile, but at least he did eventually get the thank-you notes written. It was a little painful for both of us (I had to nag; he had to listen to the nagging), but he did get them finished.

The very last place we ever want to miss manners is with our heavenly Father. Have you ever wondered if you've made a mis-step or two in your spiritual walk, but you didn't really know what it was that tripped you up? You find yourself truly desiring to go higher places in your worship, but your worship still seems a little trivial—maybe even a little elementary? Is there some joy missing too?

Maybe you've neglected an important part of entering into worship. In Psalm 100:4, the psalmist gives us a few keys to the gates of worship. We're told to enter his gates with thanksgiving and go into his courts with praise. He's referring to the gates of the temple, the same temple that represented God's high and holy presence. How were the people to access the temple and enter into the presence of their holy God? They went through the gates. And here in this passage we're told that they were to pass through those gates "with thanksgiving." Thanks!

Thanksgiving is like the doorbell into a deeper worship experi-ence with the Father. It's like an entrance into his holy presence. As we give thanks to God, we remember his faithfulness, his love, his provision, and so much more. Through thanking him, we find our focus moving from the things we think we need or the things we want God to do, to a simple place of relishing what he's already done and recognizing areas where he's at work in mighty ways. We're moved to love and adore him all the more. There's something extraordinary about a thanks-fest in the presence of God.

More Fuel in the Tank

Dwelling on all the thanks-worthy things God has done is fuel for true gladness. The first verse in Psalm 100 says to "shout with joy to the LORD" and to "worship the LORD with gladness," and to "come before him, singing with joy" (NLT). Joy, gladness, singing, and more joy! Psalm 107:21–22 says, "Let them praise the LORD for his great love and for all his wonderful deeds to them. Let them offer sacrifices of thanksgiving and sing joyfully about his glorious acts" (NLT). Our thanksgiving is a sacrifice to him. It's our offering. Even our singing is an offering.

Plug some big-time thanks into your worship and you just might find yourself ushered through the gates of his presence like never before. You can find your worship taking you to new heights. Your humble thanks brings about a worship that pleases your Father. Psalm 69:30–32 says,

> Then I will praise God's name with singing, and I will honor him with thanksgiving. For this will please the LORD more than sacrificing an ox or presenting a bull with its horns and hooves. The humble will see their God at work and be glad. Let all who seek God's help live in joy.
>
> NLT

Wow, according to these verses, you might discover new ways to live in joy.

And you just might discover new worship POW-ER (in the most gracious way)!

> Sing joyful songs to the LORD! Praise the mighty rock where we are safe. Come to worship him with thankful hearts and songs of praise. The LORD is the greatest God, king over all other gods. He holds the deepest part of the earth in his hands, and the mountain peaks belong to him. The ocean is the Lord's because he made it, and with his own hands he formed the dry land. Bow down and worship the LORD our Creator!
>
> *Psalm 95:1–6 CEV*

steppin' out when your dogs   30
are barking

Have you ever had a pair of exceptionally cute high heels, but you could hardly take a single step without a little tiny "ouch" escaping your lips? Or maybe you make that "sucking air through your teeth" sound. The choices are pretty clear in those ouch/hiss heel situations: a) leave the heels in the closet, even though they're perfect for your outfit (like that's happening), b) try to quiet the ouches—or at least get them into a rhythm so that it's musical instead of just plain annoying, or c) stuff those painful shoes with something cushy.

Some women have the baffling ability to hide the fact that their shoes are killing them. They never let the ouches slip out. How do they do that? And how are we supposed to know a friend is hurting? There are some telltale signs, subtle though they may be.

Top Ten Signs Your Friend's High Heels Are Killing Her

10. She's totally NOT gellin'.
9. Instead of "ouch/hiss," you hear Lamaze breathing.
8. You can smell Icy-Hot any time she's in the room.
7. She has the Pain Management Center on speed dial.
6. She asks for Band-Aids in a size 7½.
5. She never stands in one spot too long so the tears won't pool.
4. Her tourniquets are showing.
3. She carries a bullet in her purse so she can bite on it if the pain gets too bad.

2. She carries a cyanide pill in her purse in case the bullet doesn't work.
1. On all business forms requiring her physician's name, she lists Dr. Scholl's.

It's a 9-1-1, "paging Dr. Scholl's" kind of emergency!

What a joy it brings deep down in your sole when you add a cushy insole. It'll change your tune: from the high heel ouch/hiss song to "I've got the joy, joy, joy, joy down in my shoes!"

The joy of Jesus is like the Dr. Scholl's of this life. Joy cushions every step. It makes the pain bearable. Joy gives life bounce.

When we're experiencing pain, often our first response is to ask why. Not a bad response. Every now and then our pain is a direct result of a bad choice we've made. If a person has been unfaithful in her marriage and then experiences an excruciating breakup and the painful loss of that marriage, it's not a bad idea for her to ask why, to analyze her situation, and to see if there's repenting yet to be done.

But we don't need to get stuck in those "high heels in why places." Sometimes pain happens simply because we live in a sin-cursed, fallen world. And instead of asking "why me?" every step of a painful journey, there's joy to be found when we come to the place we can thank the Father. Thanking him through the pain requires a spiritual maturity. It's a new and high place that some people may never experience. Are you ready to step there?

Well, Under the Circumstances . . .

Joy is not about your circumstances. Your circumstances are not your life.

As children of the King, we should never find ourselves "under the circumstances." We can live in higher places. We can live OVER the circumstances! We don't need to be forever searching for conditions where the grass is greener. It's too easy to spend so much time wishing things were different that we miss all the opportunities for joy and thanksgiving—and service—right under our noses.

Paul had a great handle on it. In Philippians 4:11–13 he says,

> I have learned to be content whatever the circumstances. I know what it is to be in need, and I know what it is to have plenty. I have learned the secret of being content in any and every situation, whether well fed or hungry, whether living in plenty or in want. I can do everything through him who gives me strength.

Living in the strength of Jesus. That's living over the circumstances.

Don't let your circumstances get you down. Don't let them stifle your joy. Learn to live graciously and thankfully over and within those circumstances by the strength Christ gives. Let his strength take you to higher places. The higher places will bring peace and joy to your life, no matter what's happening around you. I've seen it happen in many lives. I've seen it happen again and again in my own life. Living in the joy of Jesus really works. Keep in mind that he has plans for you and, despite how things may seem at a painful moment, they are good plans. Jeremiah 29:11 reminds us of that again: "'I know what I am planning for you,' says the Lord. 'I have good plans for you, not plans to hurt you. I will give you hope and a good future'" (NCV). The pain you may be experiencing is not empty, fruitless pain. Our God never wastes a single ounce of our suffering. Trust him that his plan is bigger than your pain.

Sole-Searching

Let's allow pain to draw us closer to Christ—from the tips of our heads to the bottoms of our soles. Pain can remind us of the suffering he endured on our behalf, if we'll let it. Look at 1 Peter 4:12–13 again. It reminds us that experiencing pain makes us partners with Christ in his suffering.

> Dear friends, don't be surprised at the fiery trials you are going through, as if something strange were happening to you. Instead, be very glad—because these trials will make you partners with Christ in his suffering, and afterward you will have the wonderful joy of sharing his glory when it is displayed to all the world.
>
> NLT

Did you notice the "afterward" part? Joy!

Let the joy of Jesus cushion your footsteps, and you can catch yourself singing "I've got the joy, joy, joy . . . " too. And whatever happens, you can certainly forever sing, "It Is Well with My 'Sole.'"

> [You should] be exceedingly glad on this account, though now for a little while you may be distressed by trials and suffer temptations,
>
> So that [the genuineness] of your faith may be tested, [your faith] which is infinitely more precious than the perishable gold which is tested and purified by fire. [This proving of your faith is intended] to redound to [your] praise and glory and honor when Jesus Christ (the Messiah, the Anointed One) is revealed.
>
> Without having seen Him, you love Him; though you do not [even] now see Him, you believe in Him and exult and thrill with inexpressible and glorious (triumphant, heavenly) joy.
>
> *1 Peter 1:6–8 AMP*

the heels are alive 31

High heels in fast motion! I recently found a new appreciation for the beauty of the chocolate and coffee blend. Two beautiful caffeine sources in one giant mug! Sometimes I find myself appreciating them with a little too much enthusiasm. I had too many the other day, and I don't think my top eyelids touched the bottom lids for about six straight hours. I was juiced! You should've seen these heels move.

I have friends who are even more caffeine dependent than I am. One of them had a caff-attack the other day when the electricity went out. Never mind that meant there was no air-conditioning, computer or TV, refrigerator or freezer. Never mind the side of beef wasting away in there. Never mind the electric life support she was on. (Okay, kidding about the life support.) But the biggest panic about the lack of electricity had nothing to do with any of those things. It was that there was no coffeepot! I thought she was going to just chew the grounds right out of the can. Sounds like grounds for a bit of a coffee lifestyle evaluation, doesn't it? "Grounds"? Get it? Anyway, there are times I consider hooking it up intravenously too.

I know caffeine isn't really all that good for you, but I still have a hard time figuring why little old things like corpuscles and such should waste space in my caffeine system. Shouldn't we get those little suckers out of the way and make room for more mocha latte?

There's Too Much Blood in My Caffeine System

Okay, okay. I guess totally replacing a blood system with a caffeine system might not be the healthiest idea I've had. In fact, it's pretty amazing how many things I can get completely backward when I'm deciding what's good for me.

Spiritually, for instance, I can convince myself that I can get my own self revved up to serve the Lord. Not so—not even with the most concentrated caffeine. Trying to find my own direction in service, or in anything else for that matter, never takes me in the right direction. At least I find a little comfort in knowing I'm not alone. How mature is it that I have a weakness, but it makes me feel better when other people have it too? Not very! But Jeremiah 10:23 says, "O LORD, I know the way of man is not in himself; It is not in man who walks to direct his own steps" (NKJV). The right direction is just not in me. I need the God of the universe to direct my steps. He energizes my walk. That's grounds for some thanks ("grounds"—again! I'm more energized already).

Since we're in the midst of the "with joy, giving thanks to the Father" passage, I can tell you that's one of the things I'm most thankful for. He gives me purpose in life and a reason to serve, then he gives me the direction I need to go in life and in service, and then, though I'm completely inadequate, he gives me every ability I need to make it happen.

Paul agreed.

I'm so grateful to Christ Jesus for making me adequate to do this work. He went out on a limb, you know, in trusting me with this ministry. The only credentials I brought to it were invective and witch hunts and arrogance. But I was treated mercifully because I didn't know what I was doing—didn't know Who I was doing it against! Grace mixed with faith and love poured over me and into me. And all because of Jesus.

1 Timothy 1:12–14 Message

Getting Perky for Christ

Giving thanks can get our juices going. It perks the service pot. Gratitude stimulates our thinking and sets our focus on all the excellent things he has done and on all his amazing attributes. It gets us pumped and spurs us on in serving Christ. Thanksgiving is a great way to fill your heart with satisfaction and set your mind on living for Jesus to the very fullest. Want to see your high heels come alive? The heels are alive with the sound of thanking!

If you've been searching for God's will for you, this is one of his desires for you. It's crystal clear. First Thessalonians 5:18 tells us to "give thanks in all circumstances, for this is God's will for you in Christ Jesus." His will for you! Don't miss this crucial step into the worthy walk.

> I praise you, LORD, for answering my prayers. You are my strong shield, and I trust you completely. You have helped me, and I will celebrate and thank you in song. You give strength to your people, LORD, and you save and protect your chosen ones. Come save us and bless us. Be our shepherd and always carry us in your arms.

Psalm 28:6–9 CEV

There is great blessing in exercising our thanksgiving muscles, singing songs of thanks to the Father who carries us in his arms.

You can do some thanks-ercising right now. It's a great spiritual exercise to help you stay focused and fit. Stop and think about all you have to be thankful for. If we try to take credit for anything good in our lives, we're fooling ourselves. James 1:16–17 says, "Don't be deceived, my dear brothers. Every good and perfect gift is from above, coming down from the Father of heavenly lights, who does not change like shifting shadows." He has provided every one of those good things in your life. They are gifts. Thank him for every physical need he meets. Thank him for meeting your biggest needs—the spiritual, eternal ones. When you needed forgiveness, by his grace he was right there to provide it.

Thanking Him Around in Circles

It's another one of those amazing holy circles. I'm so thankful the heavenly Father has saved me through Jesus and by his grace. By that same grace he empowers me to serve him and live for him. In serving him and living for him, I find joy that compares to absolutely nothing else in this life. That joy leads me to thank my heavenly Father who has saved me through Jesus and by his grace. And so the circle goes, beginning and ending with thanks to the Father. It's all about him!

By the way, you might need to be a little careful when you're thanking him in circles. I was circle-thanking the other day, and I think I made myself a little dizzy. My husband said it wasn't really the thanks that did it. He said it was more likely that I overdid it at the coffeepot and told me I might consider decaf. I'm trying to stay in thanks mode and show gratitude for his advice. Would I sound like a smart aleck if I answered, "Yeah, thanks a latte"?

Thank you! Everything in me says "Thank you!"
Angels listen as I sing my thanks.

I kneel in worship facing your holy temple
and say it again: "Thank you!"
Thank you for your love,
thank you for your faithfulness;
Most holy is your name,
most holy is your Word.
The moment I called out, you stepped in;
you made my life large with strength.

Psalm 138:1–3 Message

light on your feet 32

One of these days I really need to learn how to travel light. As it is now, I have a suitcase for clothes, a larger suitcase for cosmetics and hair products (give me a break, I'm over forty), and an even larger suitcase for all the shoes. Every woman knows that there are specific shoes for every outfit and every occasion, and that if you try to travel without considering every possible shoe contingency, there could be cataclysmic shoe calamities. Still, every time I fly, I picture a little U-Haul with wings trailing behind the plane. Just for my shoes.

It's not only problematic when I fly, but the last time we went on the road as a family, I thought I might actually have to leave one or two of the children home so I could fit my shoe suitcase in the minivan. Kids or shoes? Kids or shoes? I finally decided to keep the kids and leave a couple of pairs of the snow boots at home. After all, it was summer.

Excess Baggage

It's not like traveling across the country with five kids isn't taxing enough. Who needs to add extra baggage to boot? We always have a great time when we travel, but I have to tell you, the trips are never without challenges.

I think the travel challenges are probably timeless, don't you? Of course, I do hope Jesus in his travels from town to town never had to say anything like, "No, Peter, I can't make John stop looking at you."

But can't you just hear Noah saying something like, "You guys better knock it off. Don't make me pull this ark over."

Or the children of Israel asking Moses for the gajillionth time, "Are we there yet?"

Or how about the head wise man (making a large leadership assumption here) on the journey to see the newborn king, "We're not stopping again. And I thought I told everybody to go before we left."

But you know, all unplanned pit stops, death glares from the front seat, and refereeing "who's looking where" aside, we're all travelers all the time, really. We're on this earth for such a short while—just passing through. We need to understand the purpose of every moment. And that purpose is in our Father through Jesus.

Take a look at 1 Peter 1:13–19 in *The Message*:

> So roll up your sleeves, put your mind in gear, be totally ready to receive the gift that's coming when Jesus arrives. Don't lazily slip back into those old grooves of evil, doing just what you feel like doing. You didn't know any better then; you do now. As obedient children, let yourselves be pulled into a way of life shaped by God's life, a life energetic and blazing with holiness. God said, "I am holy; you be holy." You call out to God for help and he helps—he's

a good Father that way. But don't forget, he's also a responsible Father, and won't let you get by with sloppy living.

Your life is a journey you must travel with a deep consciousness of God. It cost God plenty to get you out of that dead-end, empty-headed life you grew up in. He paid with Christ's sacred blood, you know. He died like an unblemished, sacrificial lamb.

Traveling with the Father

This life is a journey we must travel with a deep consciousness of God. I want to remember to make the journey in a way that honors him. He is "looking at me"—and that's okay. Remembering that my Father is looking at me, and remembering that Jesus is coming again, is motivation to roll up my sleeves and to put my mind in gear—staying ready for his coming. It has a purifying effect on my life and keeps me from getting lazy and sloppy along the journey. It's a reminder that I'm only passing through and that, as an obedient child, I need to watch out for winged U-Hauls fluttering behind me, spiritually speaking. I need to travel light.

I love the reference in Colossians 1:12 to our "Father." Make this trip alone? Hardly! The God of the universe is the Father who's at the wheel on this exciting journey.

You may have had an earthly father who was not the best driver. He may have been abusive, distant, uncaring—with baggage of his own. Don't let his baggage become yours. You have a perfect Father. He will never leave you, never fail you, never forsake you, never disappoint you, never stop caring for you in the tenderest way. "For He [God] Himself has said, I will not in any way fail you nor leave you without support. [I will] not, [I will] not, [I will] not in any degree leave you helpless nor forsake nor let [you] down (relax my hold on you)! [Assuredly not!]" (Heb. 13:5 AMP).

The Father Knows Best and Loves Best

He will never relax his loving hold on you. We don't have an impersonal God. We can call him "Father."

When the disciples asked Jesus to teach them to pray, he said, "Pray like this: Our Father in heaven . . ." (Matt. 6:9 NLT). He didn't tell them this was one of many ways to pray. He said it was *the* way to pray. He instructed them—and us—to call God "Father." It was a pretty radical concept for the disciples. Jesus called God "Father" all through his time here on earth, several times using a word that described the most intimate dad-type relationship. It was a concept of closeness the people had never known before with a holy God. A new relationship was initiated because of Jesus. We may be "stepping up" to high places, but we don't have to do it as a distant "step" child.

When you are his child, you ride ever and always in his car and under his care. You belong to him in the most loving way. It's a wondrous belonging we have in our Father! We "travel light" when we travel in his light. Psalm 56:13 says, "For you have delivered me from death and my feet from stumbling, that I may walk before God in the light of life."

He brings light to our lives. He shows us exactly where each high heel should land—or where each tire should leave its tread. He keeps us from stumbling when we ask him to do the driving. What a magnificent journey! And we're not even there yet!

> For all who are led by the Spirit of God are children of God. So you should not be like cowering, fearful slaves. You should behave instead like God's very own children, adopted into his family—calling him "Father, dear Father." For his Holy Spirit speaks to us deep in our hearts and tells us that we are God's children.
>
> *Romans 8:14–16 NLT*

part 9

"who has enabled you
to share in the saints'
inheritance in the light"

walk a mile in my pumps

I have a favorite pair of shoes that I can't seem to bring myself to rotate out of my wearing cycle. I'm experiencing "déjà shoe." They're the shoes that keep on giving. It's getting harder and harder to make them look even halfway decent, though. Scuff-arama! But they still feel so good I try not to care.

So before you judge the scuffs, you really should walk a mile in these pumps. It's not often in the high heels life you can walk a mile with a smile.

Heel, Boy

There's nothing quite like having a good ol', faithful pair of pumps lying at your feet at the end of the day. Comfy shoes instead of a dog? If you walked around in a comfy pair long enough, you might be convinced. They don't bring you the newspaper or fetch your slippers, but on the other hand, have you ever met a dog who made your legs look slimmer and who looked great with either a skirt or slacks? I rest my case.

It's not that I don't have other shoes I can wear. I've purchased plenty of new shoes since I got the comfy pair. Plenty. That's not a surprising revelation, I'm guessing. As a matter of fact, one of the most fun things about writing this book has been the juicy little detail that I could go on a shoe shopping binge and call it "research"!

Incidentally, there are likely people who would pay for the helpful research I've gathered through the *High Heels* trek. Some would pay more. Some would "Payless."

Anyway, I'm a little concerned now that I'm nearing the end of the book. How am I going to excuse my shoe shopping when the book is put to bed? Wait, I've got it. I'm thinking: sequel. How about *High Heels II: The Journey Continues*? Or maybe one of those "The Making of" volumes. *The Making of High Heels: Working on the Worthy Walk without a Net*. Maybe even a prequel. What about a "before the heels were high book" called *Baby Steps Through the Flat Lands*?

An entire extra volume just for a little authorization to do more shoe shopping? Shameless, aren't I?

Authorization Code

Here's some good news. I've been eternally authorized. Not for shoe shopping. That would force my husband to swallow large quantities of pink stomach medicine. I've been authorized to share in the Lord's inheritance. And it was God's plan for me to share in his inheritance even before the foundation of the world.

When Colossians 1:12 says that we've been "enabled" to share in the saints' inheritance, it means to be made qualified—to be authorized! I can give you the authorization code in five letters: c-r-o-s-s.

Because of the cross of Christ, we've been given his righteousness—we are saints by his power. What a huge bonus that we've also been made heirs. It's true! Romans 8:16–17 says, "The

Spirit Himself testifies together with our spirit that we are God's children, and if children, also heirs" (HCSB).

I love the way Paul tells the story in Titus 3:4–7:

> But then God our Savior showed us his kindness and love. He saved us, not because of the good things we did, but because of his mercy. He washed away our sins and gave us a new life through the Holy Spirit. He generously poured out the Spirit upon us because of what Jesus Christ our Savior did. He declared us not guilty because of his great kindness. And now we know that we will inherit eternal life.
>
> NLT

The Inheritance of Inheritances

Wouldn't it be amazing to find out we had a wealthy relative who had left us a hefty inheritance? How many shoes would THAT buy? Can we even fathom the mind-boggling truth that we have been made family with the highest of the high? There is no higher place than that place where God our Father sits. There is no higher place of importance, prominence, authority, or wealth. And when we become a child of God by grabbing on to Jesus with every ounce of strength, God becomes our legal Father. Our inheritance is from him!

First Peter 1:3–4 tells us that our inheritance will never fade. It's safe—"kept." "Praise be to the God and Father of our Lord Jesus Christ! In his great mercy he has given us new birth into a living hope through the resurrection of Jesus Christ from the dead, and into an inheritance that can never perish, spoil or fade—kept in heaven for you."

Kept by your power? My power? No, by his power. So how safe is your inheritance? It doesn't get any safer! The almighty God is your keeper every second of every day. No matter what you're doing, because of your inheritance in Christ, he keeps you tucked lovingly in the safest place.

"Trade" School

I mentioned a few chapters back that my son Jordan graduated from high school recently. We celebrated with a party in his honor. It was wonderful—except for the part where we had to clean the house. I love having a clean house. I just hate to clean it.

We've decided to try to graduate one of our kids every couple of years so that our house can get a good cleaning. We pull out the list of all the major projects we want to get done before one of these significant life event type parties. Paint, carpets, new curtains here, a new table there. Sadly, we spent so much money getting the house ready for the party that now we can't afford to send Jordan to college.

Okay, I'm just kidding. We wouldn't really trade college for curtains. That would be a worse trade than switching my comfortable pumps for a pair that's more painful and not as attractive. It's good to remember that if you're going to make a trade, make it count. Always trade up.

Trading Up

Spiritually speaking, if you've traded your sin for the righteousness of Christ, boy, have you traded up! It's trading an inheritance of iniquity, death, and hell for an inheritance of salvation, life, and heaven. That's trading way up. Up in the highest high places.

You are a loved and adored heir of God—and you are worth the life of his only Son to him. Celebrate his love for you and rejoice in your inheritance. You've traded that old way of life! While we're on the subject, trading the old way of life for a life sold out to Christ marks you as his child. You are special.

Hmm, since we're marked because of the glorious trade, I wonder if we could call that a "trade-mark." It's a trademark I'll wear happily, thanks—even more happily than my ol' faithful scuffy shoes. The *High Heels* journey really does continue.

That means the research goes on too. Roll in that truckload of pink stomach medicine for my hubby.

All honor to the God and Father of our Lord Jesus Christ, for it is by his boundless mercy that God has given us the privilege of being born again. Now we live with a wonderful expectation because Jesus Christ rose again from the dead. For God has reserved a priceless inheritance for his children. It is kept in heaven for you, pure and undefiled, beyond the reach of change and decay. And God, in his mighty power, will protect you until you receive this salvation, because you are trusting him. It will be revealed on the last day for all to see.

1 Peter 1:3–5 NLT

stepping in time   34

I had another flashback. It was a flashback of that terrible time I sank ankle deep in a mud pit in my new three-inch heels. Still haunting. I know I already shared the trauma, but did I mention the fear? I was afraid someone was going to have to come in after me. And I was afraid they might have to use scuba gear—or possibly one of those pieces of large road equipment. It was the wrong time, wrong place, wrong shoes.

I had a little revelation during my last flashback. I decided what kind of equipment would have been best. Space shoes. How handy would it have been to be able to crank up my space shoes and rocket right out of there?

Space shoes. The final frontier.

Rocket shoes could take us higher places the easy way!

Time-Altering Shoes

Maybe instead of rocket shoes, I should check into time-travel shoes. That way I could push a few buttons and—voilà!—I could travel just far enough back in time to tell myself to look down before I stepped out of the car. I could miss the mud pit episode altogether.

Time-travel shoes could get me out of a lot of other pickles too. It would be nice to have my own personal space-time continuum. At the very least I should have my own time zone. Pacific Time, Mountain Time, Central Time, Eastern Time, Revised Rhonda Time. I usually need at least an hour more than I've got for whatever I'm supposed to be doing. I often try to rev up time efficiency with a couple of those extra-large espressos. Some days, however, there just isn't a mug big enough to handle the time discrepancies.

It doesn't help that I'm frequently at least a season or two off. Last summer, for instance, I was smack in the middle of writing the Christmas book, *I'm Dreaming of Some White Chocolate*. Picture me singing carols in my Santa hat, cranking the thermostat down a few notches, and trying to be holly-jolly—all just before going out to water my petunias. When my kids caught me pulling weeds in shorts, sunglasses, and a Santa hat, they worried that the hat might have been a hair too tight. They were just sure it had already cut off some of the blood flow to the brain.

Here's a surprise. I'm in the right season today, and I don't think I've been late for anything this entire week. It's caused a little ripple in the space/time continuum. Of course, it's only Tuesday.

The Biggest Space-Time Continuum

Ecclesiastes 3:1 tells us that in the big picture, right timing is God's timing. "There is a time for everything, and a season for every activity under heaven." We're told in verse 11 that "He has made everything beautiful in its time. He has also set eternity in the hearts of men; yet they cannot fathom what God has done from beginning to end" (Message).

Our finite brains have a tough time wrapping themselves around our incredible inheritance and around what God is doing from the beginning of time to the end—even when we're not wearing hats that disrupt the blood flow. But this I do know. At the right time, God provided a way for our hearts to be clean. He provided a way for us to become saints because of Christ and to be able to spend eternity with him. Galatians 4:3–5 says,

> And that's the way it was with us before Christ came. We were slaves to the spiritual powers of this world. But when the right time came, God sent his Son, born of a woman, subject to the law. God sent him to buy freedom for us who were slaves to the law, so that he could adopt us as his very own children.
>
> NLT

In His Time

God sent his Son to be born here on earth. It's a Christmas truth that makes me want to dig out my Santa hat and wear it year-round! How glorious that the Father chose to provide salvation at just the right time. And as a little reminder, according to verses 6 and 7 of that passage, "God has sent the Spirit of his Son into your hearts, and now you can call God your dear Father. Now you are no longer a slave but God's own child" (NLT). It's the most tender "Father" love—and it's steady, unchanging, timeless!

Pondering his love and the salvation he provided revolutionizes our thinking. It changes the way we think about our time and changes the way we use it. Waste time in that old fleshly life? That plan has been revised! Revising Revised Time? Sure, we have time for that!

Don't sink back into that old way of life. It's worse than any mud pit. God has had a plan to rescue you since before time began. You don't even have to worry about being at the wrong place at the wrong time. Don't worry about the wrong shoes either. Santa boots, rocket shoes, time-travel shoes—it doesn't matter. There's a grand revised plan for your life. It's by far the biggest adventure you'll ever experience. It's the *final* final frontier.

To everything there is a season,
A time for every purpose under heaven:
A time to be born,
    And a time to die;
A time to plant,
    And a time to pluck what is planted;
A time to kill,
    And a time to heal;
A time to break down,
    And a time to build up;
A time to weep,
    And a time to laugh;

A time to mourn,
    And a time to dance;
A time to cast away stones,
    And a time to gather stones;
A time to embrace,
    And a time to refrain from embracing;
A time to gain,
    And a time to lose;
A time to keep,
    And a time to throw away;
A time to tear,
    And a time to sew;
A time to keep silence,
    And a time to speak;
A time to love,
    And a time to hate;
A time of war,
    And a time of peace.

Ecclesiastes 3:1–8 NKJV

---

take a walk on the light side 35

I've been struggling a little, thinking about that shoe section of my closet that's designated as the dark sector. It's a very large sector. Casual, dress, and extra fancy—all black. But it's because we gals have to have all varieties of black shoes to go with black pants and a black sleeveless top.

The dark pants–sleeveless top ensem is the fluffy woman's wardrobe staple. When you put all that black together, it's supposed to make some sort of mysteriously magical slimming thing happen.

I would call it "black magic," but that makes it sound too evil. On the happy, lighter side, you can put just about any color jacket on top of all the black, and somehow it works.

Life Jacket

Of course, whenever I go somewhere in my slim-suit, I can never take the jacket off. I have to hang on to the jacket for dear life. It doesn't matter what I've spilled on it. It doesn't matter what the temperature. I could be a half degree away from a heatstroke wearing all wool, and I would still have to leave the jacket on. For one thing, with all the black, if I took off the jacket, I could easily be mistaken for a cat burglar. The last thing I need is a police record. But beyond that, the jacket has a job. It covers things. Believe me; no one wants to see these upper arms. A belly view could also send those with weaker constitutions into weeks of therapy. No, the jacket is on to stay. The thing could catch fire and it's still not coming off.

It is a little embarrassing that I have a houseful of teenagers, yet I'm the one who looks a little Goth. Space shoes are one thing, but I think I've gone over to the dark side.

The Force Is Strong with This One

Sometimes I get a little embarrassed in anticipation of the time when I've gone on to glory and someone else is left to go through the dark side of my closet. I can just hear them saying something like, "What? Was she *always* in mourning?"

But while there is often so much black covering the outside of me, inside there is the best kind of light. Thankfully, I don't have to generate it. It's a different side of the force—the real and divine force of our holy God.

The "light" in Colossians 1:12 suggests "divine truth." Psalm 119:130 says, "The unfolding of your words gives light; it gives understanding to the simple." The light can also refer to God's kind of divine purity. Ephesians 5:8–14 says,

> For you were once darkness, but now you are light in the Lord. Live as children of light (for the fruit of the light consists in all goodness, righteousness and truth) and find out what pleases the Lord. Have nothing to do with the fruitless deeds of darkness, but rather expose them. For it is shameful even to mention what the disobedient do in secret. But everything exposed by the light becomes visible, for it is light that makes everything visible. This is why it is said: "Wake up, O sleeper, rise from the dead, and Christ will shine on you."

Think about our inheritance! Truth and purity—light!

Our inheritance is also heaven. "Light" refers to God's kingdom. God's plan for our future includes that glorious kingdom to come. In Matthew 25:34, we find that Jesus will say, "Come, you who are blessed by my Father; take your inheritance, the kingdom prepared for you since the creation of the world."

There will be no mourning in that place. I guess that means I'll have to have a whole new wardrobe—and I'm so perfectly okay with that! There won't be a single corner of darkness in heaven because the light of Jesus will fill every nook and cranny. Revelation 21:23 tells us that "the city does not need the sun or the moon to shine on it, for the glory of God gives it light, and the Lamb is its lamp." Jesus will be our perfect light in the glorious future we've inherited.

Strolling in the Light

He is our light in the here and now too. Second Corinthians 4:6 says, "For God, who said, 'Let light shine out of darkness,' made his light shine in our hearts to give us the light of the knowledge of the glory of God in the face of Christ." Jesus himself said in John 8:12, "I am the light of the world. Whoever follows me will never walk in darkness, but will have the light of life."

Walking in his light is walking worthy—and it can happen in those cute high heels. Any shoes. Dark shoes, light shoes, or no shoes. With Jesus you will never, never, never walk in darkness. If you are his, you're not built for darkness. Your Father wants the very best for you—his light.

Our enemy, Satan, is darkness. That's where sin and everything ugly is. The enemy wants to trip you up in your worthy walk. But don't fear him. Simply refuse him. All you have to do to avoid darkness is to step into the light. That's Jesus! Keep your eyes on Christ and keep your heart obediently trusting him and his Word. "If you are filled with light, with no dark corners, then your whole life will be radiant, as though a floodlight is shining on you" (Luke 11:36 NLT).

Let his floodlight shine on you. I can't begin to tell you what contentment you'll find.

And I'm assuming I don't need to tell you how his floodlight compares to a blazing jacket. There is no comparison. I want his floodlight. Not a "smoking jacket."

This is the message which we have heard from Him and declare to you, that God is light and in Him is no darkness at all. If we say that we have fellowship with Him, and walk in darkness, we lie and do not practice the truth. But if we walk in the light as He is in the light, we have fellowship with one another, and the blood of Jesus Christ His Son cleanses us from all sin.

1 John 1:5–7 NKJV

pedi-cured

I've always wished I was a pedicure kind of gal. I have one big pedicure obstacle: overly ticklish feet. If I could get a pedicure without anyone ever actually touching my feet, it would be perfect.

I've heard from friends that there's nothing quite like it. It's an ankles-down spa. They say a pedicure gives you totally new feet.

Need to know if you need new feet? Here are some signs it's time to put a pedicure at the top of your to-do list.

Top Ten Signs You Need a Pedicure

10. Your high heels disintegrate.
9. The pedicurist refuses to do the work on you with anything besides her three-foot tongs.
8. You can't get your pantyhose past your feet without shredding them.
7. Instead of cotton balls between your toes, the pedicure team decides ball bearings should hold up better.
6. You go out to the mailbox barefoot and on your way back discover that every place you stepped you killed the grass.
5. You step on a tack and it takes you two weeks to notice.
4. At the fancy Japanese restaurant, you're the only one who's asked to put her shoes back on.
3. Your hubby asks if you'll sharpen his circular saw by running the bottom of your feet across the blade a few times . . . and when you do, you see sparks.
2. Every time you do make it in for a pedicure, they put you in a half-hour kerosene soak first.

1. The shoe salesperson removes your shoes then abruptly decides to join the Foreign Legion.

If after your last pedicure you noticed you were wearing a size smaller shoe, then it's a good clue you need to stay on top of the pedicure situation. Then again, if after your last pedicure, the pedicurist suddenly up and decided to become a forest ranger—that's probably an even better sign you need to stay a little more pedi-ready.

I don't know about you, but my feet could use a good polishing. As a matter of fact, my whole body could use a good polishing. Is there a full-body pedicure?

Remodeling Project

At least I had a little "face-i-cure" recently when I did a TV interview. The makeup is always my favorite part. It's not a total face cure, but it is like getting a little makeover. But should I be offended that it took a solid half hour to do the makeup? "We're just enhancing what's already here," she kept saying. Never mind that she was mixing the makeup with something that looked like a tiny trowel. Enhancing? I think it was more of a remodel job. I'm just glad she fought off any urges to yell something like, "Hey, Harv! We're going to need the belt sander, some heavy-duty mortar, and an extra nail gun!"

Not that I would have stopped her. There are times I would be perfectly content with a bit of a remodel. Especially since my foundation seems to have settled a little. I have to wonder about my structural integrity. A little brick work, a little landscaping, maybe a Sheetrock repair or two might just work wonders on this old house. After all, somewhere along the way I seemed to have picked up a few more bricks than my foundation could comfortably hold. I even asked the makeup lady about knocking off a few of these chins, but she just laughed.

How about a Life Remodel?

Our journey to higher places wouldn't be complete without asking if you feel you need a life remodel. Need a new addition here, a revamping there?

The life remodel begins with understanding God's amazing love for you. It's a very personal love. You are his treasure—his delight. Because of Jesus, you can enter into the holy presence of God and enjoy his love and acceptance. Because of Christ, you have access to the very heart of God. Could there be any higher place?

Maybe you've strayed from the original blueprint, spiritually speaking. It's easy to feel that way any time we lose focus of our real purposes in life. Often taking your next step in your walk with Christ is merely understanding that this fellowship is available to you. Want more of God? Think about, dwell on, bask in his love for you!

If you've never surrendered your life to him in the first place, that's your first step. It's a step every single person in this world must take to become a child of the Father. Every person needs the Savior, Jesus. Since sin entered the world in the Garden of Eden, we've all been separated from a holy God—with absolutely no hope of going higher on our own. There's no cleaning up our own lives. And there is not a one of us who doesn't need the cleanup. Every one of us since the beginning has sinned. Romans 3:10–11 says, "There is no one righteous, not even one; there is no one who understands, no one who seeks God."

But God had a loving plan. Romans 5:8 says that "God demonstrates his own love for us in this: While we were still sinners, Christ died for us." Jesus lived a sinless life and died a sacrificial death on the cross to pay our sin penalty. "For all have sinned and fall short of the glory of God, and are justified freely by his grace through the redemption that came by Christ Jesus. God presented him as a sacrifice of atonement, through faith in his blood" (Rom. 3:23–25). Redemption came by Christ Jesus!

When Jesus died on the cross, he took the punishment for every sin you've ever committed—past, present, and future—and when you surrender to him, you are declared righteous in the eyes of God. Romans 3:22 tells us that "this righteousness from God comes through faith in Jesus Christ to all who believe."

You Can Bet Your Life!

Three days after Jesus died, he rose from the dead, conquering sin and death once and for all. Victory! If you will ask him to forgive your sin and come into your life and if you will surrender control to him, he will forgive. You can trust the promise of Romans 10:13: "Everyone who calls on the name of the Lord will be saved." As a matter of fact, you can trust in that promise with your life!

Are you ready to trust? Have you been running your life yourself? If so, I can guess that you've made a pretty big mess of things—and I'll guess you're fed up with it all. I'll also venture to say that it's no accident that the Lord brought you to this time and this place—and this page. If you're ready to trade the fed-up life for one of joy and peace and purpose, surrender to his plan for you. Get in on the abundant, eternal life! You can pray something like this:

> Lord, I'm fed up—and I know it's because I've messed up. I've broken your laws. Would you please forgive me? I believe you died on the cross to pay for everything wrong I've ever done. I believe you rose again, victorious over sin and death. I trust you right now to forgive every sin—to give me a total makeover of the soul. Thank

you for forgiving me. Thank you for your amazing and personal love for me that's at the heart of that forgiveness. I give you my life—absolutely all of it. Lord, take me to higher places; make me more and more like Jesus. Use me in any and every way that will bring glory and honor to you. Use me all the rest of my life. Thank you for saving me. In Jesus' name, Amen.

Did you know that from the very moment you ask for his forgiveness and give him your life, he makes you brand new? It's better than a remodel. It's better than new feet. It's a brand-new you! Sin is cured—forever!

If you just prayed that prayer for the first time, let someone know what's going on in your life. Let a solid believer help you as you get started in your new walk with Christ. Let them help you find out more and more what this worthy walk is about. And let me be the first to welcome you to this most magnificent life!

The remodeling transformation continues as we allow the Holy Spirit to do his work in our lives. It's growth in the worthy walk. Second Corinthians 3:17–18 says,

> Now, the Lord is the Spirit, and wherever the Spirit of the Lord is, he gives freedom. And all of us have had that veil removed so that we can be mirrors that brightly reflect the glory of the Lord. And as the Spirit of the Lord works within us, we become more and more like him and reflect his glory even more.
>
> NLT

Now there's a makeover! Through the Holy Spirit we can have a heart makeover that's perpetual—constantly building structural integrity of the soul. And that's real integrity. Even better, when the makeup job is finished and we're ready to look into the mirror, guess who we'll see. Jesus! As we allow the Spirit to do his makeover work in our lives, we become more and more like our

Savior. How perfectly beautiful to have the mirror reflecting HIS glory! It's a life makeover that gives us ever-increasing joy.

Higher Happiness

So many women have the idea that the higher walk means a happy walk. It's true that your heavenly Father wants you to be happy. Even every good earthly father wants to see his children happy and does everything he can to make it happen. The Father truly does want you to walk worthy with great joy. He even commands it in Philippians 4:4: "Always be full of joy in the Lord. I say it again—rejoice!" (NLT). We need to pick up his joy and faithfully walk in it. Walking in his joy is walking in his will.

I must say, though, if you picked up this book to go higher places in happiness, you may not have gotten what you expected. A person who seeks happiness is not usually the one who finds it. But a person who seeks Jesus with a whole and sincere heart finds a happiness she wasn't necessarily even seeking. Trust Jesus, believe him, follow him, and you can find happiness you didn't even know you were looking for. Yes, there's a happiness makeover in those higher places with him too!

Summing up the joy-filled, worthy walk of maturity would be incomplete without God's idea of beautiful feet—not necessarily those that are polished and corn-free (by the way, I'm glad I never promised this book would be corn-free). A worthy walk is full of instructions to "stand," to "walk," and to "run." Even the armor of God has the preparation of the gospel of peace where? On the feet! The higher life is for those who are mature enough to share his good news. Jesus showed us how to be mature, humble servants when he washed a roomful of dirty disciple feet in that holy pedicure of all pedicures.

And the Trip Goes On

I hope you're thanking the Father with me for this journey. What a trip! I'm completely sincere, too, when I give you my heartfelt thanks for taking the trip with me. The Lord has had some wonderful surprises through it all. I'm praying for you and for me, that our *High Heels* journey won't stop with the last page of this book. We should ever and always be aspiring to go higher with him.

We don't serve a simple God. We can spend our entire lives getting to know him and still have more to know. It's incredible. We step up to a higher place and find the inexpressible joy there of a higher place after that one! Higher still!

> Dear Lord, thank you for every little changed place in every heart all along this *High Heels* journey—all by your power and for your glory! Oh Lord, don't let us stop now! Father, take us higher still!

Let's keep the journey going! Let's continue to go to those higher and holier places with him.

Take off your high heels. This is holy ground. (Since you have to take your shoes off, I do hope you've had a pedicure!)

> For God in all his fullness was pleased to live in Christ, and by him God reconciled everything to himself. He made peace with everything in heaven and on earth by means of his blood on the cross. This includes you who were once so far away from God. You were his enemies, separated from him by your evil thoughts and actions, yet now he has brought you back as his friends. He has done this through his death on the cross in his own human body. As a result, he has brought you into the very presence of God, and you are holy and blameless as you stand before him without a single fault. But you must continue to believe this truth and stand in it firmly.
>
> *Colossians 1:19–23 NLT*

notes

1. Jennifer Rothschild, eNewsletter, www.WomensMinistry.NET, 2/28/06. Jennifer Rothschild is author of *Lessons I Learned in the Dark* and founder of Womens Ministry Network.

2. Wellington Boone, *Breaking Through* (Nashville: Broadman & Holman, 1996), 132–33. Used by permission.

3. "Footprints of Jesus," words by Mary Slade.

4. Andrew Murray, "The Milk of the Word" (ch. 2), *Words of God for Young Disciples of Christ,* from Christian Classics Ethereal Library, www.ccel.org.

5. Andrew Murray, *With Christ in the School of Prayer* (Gainesville, FL: Bridge-Logos, 1999), xix–xx.

6. Ibid.

7. Kaley Faith Rhea, "The Gift," 2005. Used by permission.

discussion guide

You Take the High Road, I'll Take the . . . No, Wait, Let's ALL Take the High Road Together!

Would you like to take a step or two toward a closer walk with Christ? If you're picking up this discussion guide for your own personal study time, that's wonderful. Skip the "Discussion Kickoff" prompts and dive right into the questions for each chapter. There are just a small handful of group-focused questions, but they're easily tweakable to fit your personal reflection time. You'll find most of them adapt well for individual application as you step toward higher places.

If you're picking up this discussion guide for group discussion, well, what could be more fun and fruitful than taking the journey through *High Heels in High Places* with a group of girlfriends? Strap on your heels! We're heading higher!

Notes for the Discussion Leader

Taking a group with you on the *High Heels* journey? Spectacular! This discussion guide should be just the ticket to give you hints and helps as you encourage women to apply truths from God's Word about the worthy walk and about learning to walk it out. How glorious it is when women can set a higher goal rather than merely reading a book. The higher goal? Getting personal, making it real, taking it to heart. Higher, higher, higher places!

High Heels in High Places is a step-by-step walk through Colossians 1:9–12. Isn't it magnificent that as we look at God's Word, he can change us in such dramatic, life-altering ways? Watching women change right before your eyes, to the glory of God—could it get any sweeter? We'll be looking at the Colossians passage phrase by phrase. There are four chapters for every phrase and nine sections in all.

If you would like to plan a 10-week study, you can take one section per week. If you're able to take it a little slower, you'll find more opportunities for sharing more deeply. A chapter per week would be ideal, though you may find some women may be a little reluctant to make a 37-week commitment (36 chapters plus the introduction). Happily, anyone should be able to jump in at any time during the study. And also, there's really no wrong way to take your group on the *High Heels* journey. You'll likely find a schedule that will fit your needs and your group's needs.

These personal reflection questions are designed to help us think about and fruitfully process what we've seen in God's Word. Each chapter begins with a "Discussion Kickoff" designed to help women loosen up and laugh. Sharing on a surface level can break down barriers and free group members to later share on a deeper, more significant level. Prepare an answer or story for the kickoff in case, as the leader, you might need to "kickoff the kickoff," so to speak. Several of the kickoffs have some sort of award, trophy, or certificate—add your own award to the other weeks, if you like. For a real hoot, put together (or ask a helper to put together) a homemade award for the best story. You'll be surprised when you see how much the women look forward to those kickoff awards. If you take photos of the recipients and their awards each week, you can display them all in a hilarious remembrance at your last *High Heels* group meeting.

As the discussion leader, you'll need to find that tricky balance of sharing enough of yourself on every level to allow your group to trust you, but not so much that you make the discussion too much about you. If you have a close friend in the group, make yourself accountable to her and ask her to honestly tell you if you're hitting that balance well.

I encourage you to make it your goal to always be transparent. If you are real—even with your struggles—your group will most often respect your genuineness and they will feel freer to share their own struggles as they come up.

What You'll Need to Do Each Week

Encourage your group to read the assigned chapter or chapters before the group meeting, but let them know that they won't feel out of place there if they get behind in reading. Reminders through phone calls or emails are great. You can divvy up those duties, or ask one of your group members if they would consider being a contact person. Even with a contact person, as the group leader, it's great to check in on your group whenever you can. Ask each one how you may pray for her.

As you're going through the week's assigned reading, make a few notes or observations you would like to point out or comment on during that week's discussion time. If the Lord teaches you something poignant, confronts you on an issue, or deeply moves you in some way, openly share that with your group.

May I also encourage you to make a weekly commitment to pray for each of your group members? What life-changing power there is in prayer!

After you've done the assigned readings and prayed for your group, look over the discussion questions. Be ready to offer some answers if the discussion needs a little charge, but again, be careful not to monopolize the chat time.

It's always fun, though certainly not mandatory, to have some snacks to offer. You can call for volunteers or put something together yourself. Doesn't chocolate almost always speak to women in a profound way? I've heard it said that good chocolates are like shoes. You can never have just one.

Discussion Group Rules

You'll want to set up some ground rules for the group from the very first meeting. Here are some suggestions:

* Personal information shared within the group does not leave the group. Remind each other regularly that everyone should be able to freely share and know that no one in the group will ever betray a confidence.
* If someone shares a need or asks for prayer during a meeting, someone should volunteer right then to stop and pray for that need. Just a few sentences will be perfect.
* No cutting remarks or unkind comments to anyone in the group or about anyone outside the group. Uplifting, positive words only.
* Likewise, never correct anyone in front of the group. Belittling or embarrassing someone into changed behavior rarely works. If confrontation is necessary, it should be done in private and always in love.

* If someone says something contrary to God's Word, however, let her know you respect her opinion, but also let her know, in a loving manner, what the Bible does say. His truth needs to be our bottom line on every issue, and every group discussion should reflect that.

Prayers for You!

Thank you again for taking on the role of discussion leader. You're making a difference in the Kingdom! Now may I pray for you?

Father, thank you for the discussion leader's availability to be used by you to touch the lives of women. I ask that you would bless her in the most marvelous way for her sacrifice of service. Lord, let her find joy in this journey that absolutely surprises her. May she come to know those in her group in a deeper way. May she see the lives of women changed by your power right before her very eyes. Would you please bring exactly the right women into her group? If there are any who don't know you in the most personal way, would you even now be drawing them to yourself? I ask that you would grant the discussion leader great wisdom from you and insight into your Word. Grant her the sacrificial, Jesus-kind of love for each woman in her group. Knit hearts together as only you can do. Move and work in the lives of women in whatever way will bring you the most glory. Oh, Lord, would you please take the leader, the group, all of us, to higher places with you! In Jesus' name, Amen.

discussion guide

Introduction: "We are asking . . ."

Discussion Kickoff: What is the weirdest shoe purchase you've ever made? Who wins the shoe trophy for the most ridiculous amount of shoes?

1. There's nothing like spending time in God's Word. Take another look at Colossians 1:9–12. Paul is asking for some big things in this passage—some "high" things. Are there some high things you're ready to ask God to do in your life through the time you spend in this book? Are you willing to write them out or share them with your group?

2. Can you think of a time when you sensed the Father working in your life and you knew without a doubt you were heading to higher places? If so, what did the Lord use to point you to that richer walk?

3. Is that something you would like to see happen in your life again? Or if you've never experienced it, would you like to? Are you ready to seek a higher walk? Ready to ask BIG? Pray through the prayer at the end of the introduction. Ask BIG!

Part 1 *"that you may be filled with the knowledge of his will"*

Chapter 1: It's All About the Shoes

Discussion Kickoff: Have you ever found something strange, gross, or *living* in one of your shoes? Before or after the foot went in?

1. What's the first thing we need to do if we want to be filled with the knowledge of his will? Have you ever done that?
2. Is there any "emptying" you need to do? Have you caught sight of any of those worldly philosophies, sneaky lies, sinful habits, or selfish thoughts that you need to get rid of? Will you take the time to pray through those things today?
3. Are you ready to ask the Lord to fill you up with himself? What does it mean to let him fill you? What differences does it make in your life when you're filled up with him?

Chapter 2: Foot-notes

Discussion Kickoff: Has anyone ever tried to tackle you over a clearance bargain? What's the most bizarre shopping scene you've ever witnessed?

1. Are you truly seeking the knowledge of the Lord's will? Are you willing to ask him to help you stay true to seeking his will and not your own?
2. How desperate are you for his filling? Are you willing to do absolutely anything it takes? What do you think that kind of willingness could cost a person?

3. What kind of worthy walk will there be for you if you're not willing to do whatever it takes? How different is that from the filled-up, worthy walk?

Chapter 3: What's Your Shoe Size?

Discussion Kickoff: Did your Barbie have more shoes than you did? Who wins the Barbie trophy for the funniest Barbie-related story?

1. Have you ever caught yourself unconsciously measuring right and wrong with a measuring stick other than the Word of God? What erroneous standards do you see others using to measure truth?
2. What is your own personal "next step" in studying God's Word?
3. Look at the passage at the end of the chapter. According to Psalm 119:34–35, what can we find along the path of God's commands? Could you use more of it?

Chapter 4: Wake Up, Step Up, Pray Up

Discussion Kickoff: Has anything painfully embarrassing ever happened to you at an exercise class? Have you ever seen anything painfully embarrassing happen to someone else?

1. Are you as committed to prayer and as convinced of its earth-shaking power as you'd like to be? Have you ever heard of anyone who has experienced sweet, intimate fellowship with God the Father without prayer?

2. Under the subhead "The Prayer Necessities," Romans 12:12 lists three instructions. What are they and how do the three tie together?
3. Are there new ways you might like to build some muscle in your prayer life? Have you considered making yourself accountable to someone else?

Part 2 *"in all wisdom and spiritual understanding"*

Chapter 5: Baby Steps Are for . . . Well . . . Babies

Discussion Kickoff: "The White Shoe Award" goes to anyone who can accurately explain which color shoes are off-limits in which seasons. What's the most disturbing way you've ever seen a pair of shoes bite the dust?

1. What does it mean to obey God?
2. If you are a follower of Christ, how has living in obedience to him changed your life?
3. Are there higher places you would like to go in living a life of obedience? Are you ready to look into his eyes and say, "Oh yes, Lord! I want to follow you!"

Chapter 6: The Shoe's on the Other Foot

Discussion Kickoff: What's the worst shoe counsel you've ever received? Hair counsel? The "Hilariously Horrible Hair Award" goes to the one with the funniest bad hair experience.

1. Can you see a powerful connection between maturing in the Lord, walking worthy in him, and depending on him more fully? What does it mean to depend on him? What

does a person's life look like when she is fully depending on the Lord?

2. Under the "Dependence is In" section, dependence is compared to what? How does that apply to you?

3. Are you ready and willing to pray a prayer of complete dependence? Read Psalm 131:1–2 under the "Mercy Me" section again.

Chapter 7: Heels on Wheels

Discussion Kickoff: What's the weirdest thing you've ever found in your car? The most disgusting? Who wins the "Auto Albatross Award"?

1. Have you ever known someone who wanted wisdom and understanding and a higher walk with the Lord, but refused to let go of a blatant sin issue? Were they able to achieve a high life while still hanging on to that sin?

2. Are there times when you've chosen "the hard way" when it comes to sin? According to the section "Changing Direction," how many steps does it take to head in the right direction?

3. The question is asked, "Are you aching to have freedom from sin and a new closeness to your Heavenly Father in those higher places with him?" How are we instructed to take the step out of that ache and into the Promised Land? If you haven't in a while, are you ready to ask him to forgive you and clean you up on the inside?

Chapter 8: Step Off, Girlfriend!

Discussion Kickoff: Has anything wacky ever made its way inside your house? One of your friends' houses? Who might win the "Top the Bird in the House Story" trophy?

1. Have you ever found yourself thinking you've got it all together and you can plan out your life on your own? Where does that kind of thinking usually take you? What does Proverbs 16:9 say about it?
2. Do you believe it's true that God can use our humility to give us confidence? Can you cite a time when that has happened in your life?
3. According to Colossians 2:2–3, where do we find all the treasures of wisdom and knowledge? What is God's secret plan? How does that apply to the first question?

Part 3 *"so that you may walk worthy of the Lord, fully pleasing to him"*

Chapter 9: There Was an Old Woman Who Lived . . . Where?

Discussion Kickoff: Have you ever experienced one of those embarrassing "wrong shoe" moments? Can you tell about the time when you laughed the most inappropriately? Can you tell it without giggling?

1. Have you asked yourself why you might desire the "wisdom and spiritual understanding" we looked at in the last section? Do you think we ever desire those things so that we

can impress others? What is the reason God would want us to have this knowledge, as explained in Colossians 1:10?

2. In the section "Where Can We Find Passion?" we're told how to find a constant connection to the Father, how to passionately draw near to him. What do we need to do to find that connection?

3. Are you willing to commit to doing those things? Are you even willing to make yourself accountable to someone if you need to, asking that person to ask you on a regular basis how you're doing in those areas?

Chapter 10: Don't Try Walking with Your Shoes on the Wrong Feet

Discussion Kickoff: What's the weirdest thing you've ever had to clean out of your family room? What's the strangest thing you've ever had to clean out of your vacuum cleaner? Could you win the "Vacuum's Biggest Sucker Award"?

1. What are some of the ways we tend to let our minds suck up the wrong things?

2. According to Philippians 4:8, what are we supposed to fill our minds with instead?

3. Are there issues from your past that might be clogging your worthy walk? Are there sins you've confessed but still haunt you with guilt? Do you believe Jesus is big enough to forgive and cleanse you? Are there issues from your past in which you were the victim? Are you ready to deal with those things, get one-on-one counseling where you need to, forgive, and start looking toward the future?

Chapter 11: Scratching Where It Itches with Athlete's Foot

Discussion Kickoff: Have you ever experienced a "running in high heels" disaster? Other running disasters?

1. Have you ever sung your own version of the Romans 7:21–25 song? According to that passage, how do we win struggles against sin?
2. What usually happens when people try to fight a temptation in their own strength? What should you do if you're tempted when a certain TV show is on, when you're on the Internet, or when you're in the company of a particular person?
3. What should every follower of Christ run from and who should every follower run to? Are you running in the right direction? What are some practical things you can do to start heading in the right direction or to keep going in the right direction?

Chapter 12: Keep on Walking

Discussion Kickoff: Have you ever learned a painful lesson in an exercise class? Who might win "The Biggest Pain" certificate of recognition?

1. What is it that makes a solid spiritual core and a worthy walk? Can you think of a person in your life who is a good example to you of that kind of walk?
2. What do you think truly pleases the Father?
3. How are you doing at "keeping the ball rolling"? Are you ready to commit to the worthy walk and to commit to keep

on walking it? What do you think it might take for you to achieve this?

Part 4 *"bearing fruit in every good work"*

Chapter 13: Step Lightly and Carry a Big Purse

Discussion Kickoff: Do you have a strange combination of items in your purse? Do you carry one of those ten-ton handbags? Are you willing to compete in a purse weigh-off for the "Biggest Bag" prize?

1. What are the spiritual fruits that grow out of a worthy walk?
2. Is there someone in your life who models a life of faith? How has that influenced your life?
3. Do you think you might be that kind of model to someone else?

Chapter 14: Fashion Footed

Discussion Kickoff: What's the most bizarre extreme you've gone to so you could get your hands on a soft drink, a cup of coffee, a hunk of chocolate, or whatever it is that satisfies your own personal craving or obsession?

1. What are some of the strange cravings and obsessions we see in people all around us? What kind of cravings and obsessions might we be passing along to those around us?
2. According to Isaiah 52:7, what is God's description of beautiful feet? What are some tangible blessings we receive when we share the Good News of Jesus Christ?

3. Would you be willing to write down on paper a testimony of what Jesus means to you and what he's done in your life? Are you ready to share it?

Chapter 15: Get Your Footing

Discussion Kickoff: Describe an athletic "train wreck" you or someone you know has experienced. Can you name a time when you felt the absolute wimpiest? Any unsual ways you've had to "feel the burn"?

1. Can you feel the burn in your spiritual life? Are you stretching spiritually? What are some new ways we can stretch ourselves in the worthy walk?
2. According to 1 Corinthians 12:7, who has received a spiritual gift? Can you name a spiritual gift you've been given? If you don't know, how might you go about finding out? Name some practical ways to fan the flames of your own spiritual gift.
3. A fruit assignment is given in this chapter right from the Word of God (Philippians 1:9–10). What is that assignment? What are some specific ways you can do your part?

Chapter 16: Put on Your Dancing Tennies

Discussion Kickoff: Have you ever had a klutzy pet? What is the funniest disaster you've ever seen perpetrated by an animal?

1. What kind of fruit do you love to see in the lives of others? In your own life?

2. As you find yourself drawing closer to the heavenly Father, do you notice him pointing out areas of sin in your life that you never noticed before?

3. Taking care of those areas of sin is growth in the worthy walk, growth in the "higher places" kind of life. Will you stop sometime today and ask God to show you those pesky sin places, confess them, get rid of them, and let him take you higher still?

Part 5 *"and growing in the knowledge of God"*

Chapter 17: A Step and a Squish

Discussion Kickoff: Could you be the winner of the "Worst Combination of Babies and Shoes Ever Award"?

1. Have you ever met a person who refused to change? What kind of life did that person have?

2. Ephesians 4:22–24 gives us instructions in how to experience great change. What does the passage say we should do? How are you doing in applying it? Are you ready to grow?

3. What do you see as your very deepest need? How do you think you can see that need met?

Chapter 18: Lessons for Loafers

Discussion Kickoff: What's the most embarrassing thing you've ever had to shove into hiding when you had company coming? What's the most embarrassing thing you never had a chance to hide before surprise guests arrived?

1. Do you feel you've taken any steps higher in your spiritual walk since starting this study? Are you ready to see what God has in mind for your "next, next step"?
2. What are some practical ways everyone can grow in studying God's Word? Grow in prayer? Grow in knowledge?
3. Are there some specific steps you personally can take in each of these areas?

Chapter 19: Some Fancy Footwork

Discussion Kickoff: What are some of the goofy shoe styles you've worn in the past? Do you have pictures to incriminate yourself? Can you describe the absolute strangest pair of shoes you've ever seen? Do you have one you can bring and show off to the group?

1. Is your life of surrender as much about being a blessing as it is about receiving a blessing? Describe the difference.
2. What hindrances to blessing do self-promotion, self-indulgence, and self-centeredness cause?
3. What exactly do we find as we let go of self and grab on to surrender? Have you ever done that? If not, are you willing to now?

Chapter 20: Sometimes Sandals Are the Best High Heels

Discussion Kickoff: Do you have more shoes than you have cooking utensils? Are you still up for more shoe shopping? Could you be the winner of the "Shop 'Til EVERYBODY Drops Award" for the longest shopping marathon?

1. As you know the Lord better and better, what happens to your faith? Why do you think that is?
2. Based on that, what can you do to intentionally build and grow your faith? Get specific.
3. What looks different about the life of a person whose faith is continually growing? If you haven't already, would you like to see that kind of difference in your own life? What do you need to do?

Part 6 *"may you be strengthened with all power, according to his glorious might"*

Chapter 21: Waiting for the Other Shoe to Drop

Discussion Kickoff: Is there a particularly creative Solomon-like parent judgment you've witnessed? Did your parents ever hand down a doozy? Have you?

1. What are some distracting battles people can find themselves fighting? Are there any unworthy battles you've fought in the past? How do those kinds of battles affect our ability to walk worthy in the Lord?
2. Who is our enemy? How does he use senseless battles as distracting potholes? What should we do about it?
3. What is the "good fight"? How can we fight it? What is the outcome? Are you committed to fighting the good fight?

Chapter 22: Shoe Box Faith

Discussion Kickoff: Could you be the winner of the "Most Creative Use of a Shoe Box Award"? If you had made a box into a time capsule when you were six years old, what would you have put in it?

1. What kinds of fruitless gifts do people tend to think they can offer God? Do those kinds of offerings strengthen a person's life?
2. Where does a well placed faith rest? Is yours perfectly at rest?
3. Look at the passage at the end of the chapter. According to Ephesians 3:16–19, what is the basis of the strength the Lord gives? Will you decide today to pray to the loving God who truly wants to give you real inner strength?

Chapter 23: Step Up to the Gate

Discussion Kickoff: What's the worst stench you've ever come across inside your house? Would you be in the running in the eye-watering competition for the "Ultimate Stink-Off" trophy?

1. What spiritual aspects of their lives do you see people often trying to control? How does that seem to work out for them?
2. Think about the power of God. What are some of the ways his strength is described in Ephesians 1:19–22?
3. Do you need to take a little stress out of your life? Striving to run things in our own strength is a huge source of frustration and stress. Are you ready to trust the one who has all the strength? Are you ready to ask him, the all-powerful, ever-strong one, for the kind of strength that counts? How could that affect your worthy walk?

Chapter 24: You Put Your Right Foot In

Discussion Kickoff: What's the goofiest diet you've ever heard about? What's the goofiest diet you've ever tried?

1. What does it mean to put our thinking on the altar? How can that change a life? How long has it been since you've surrendered your thought life to God? Are you ready to do it?
2. Ephesians 4:1–3 tells us the worthy walk is a calling. What does it mean to be called?
3. In the section titled, "Calling All Worthy Walkers," we're told there's something important that comes with a calling. What is it? Are you willing to let the Lord give you what you need in order to do what he's called you to do?

Part 7 *"for all endurance and patience"*

Chapter 25: Check the Bottom of Your Shoe

Discussion Kickoff: Have you ever found anything especially bizarre stuck to your shoe? Have you ever seen anything bizarre inside someone's car?

1. What are some of the things people tend to worry about? How does the worry help? How does it hurt?
2. When was the last time you did a "worry exam"? Are there any worries threatening your joy right now?
3. What does Philippians 4:6–8 tell us to do instead of worrying? Will you commit to doing it? Are you ready to start today?

Chapter 26: Shoes That Work in a Pinch

Discussion Kickoff: What's the most creative thing you've seen a woman do to ease the discomfort of a painful pair of cute shoes? Could you win the "Origami-Feet Story Award"?

1. Have you ever experienced a difficulty that you later saw God use as an opportunity for growth and maturity in your life?
2. Are you experiencing a struggle right now? If so, have you found yourself wondering where God is in the midst of your struggle?
3. How can you answer the "Where is God?" question after reading this chapter and looking at the Scriptures? Can you apply that answer in the most personal way, no matter what difficulties you may experience? How might leaning on some Christian sisters lighten your load?

Chapter 27: Stepping-Stones Can Break Your Bones

Discussion Kickoff: Do you think your idea of "comfort food" might be considered a little strange? When the road is rocky, what is your "Rocky Road"?

1. When you're experiencing a difficulty, is your very first prayer often, "Oh God, get me out of this!"?
2. What might we miss if we try to squirm out of difficulties too quickly?
3. Describe the hope you find when you compare the temporary struggle to the everlasting joy. How does it affect your worthy walk?

Chapter 28: Take a Stroll with Your Mat

Discussion Kickoff: What is the wildest mess you've ever had to clean up? Do you think you might be the winner of the "Wild, Wild Mess Award"?

1. Have you ever met a person who was very bitter? How did it affect this person? Did the person's bitterness affect other relationships and other aspects of life? How?
2. When the topic of dealing with difficult people crops up, is there a face that immediately pops to your mind? Is there any bitterness you might be hanging on to? If so, are you ready to be free of it? What do you need to do to make this happen? Even if the person or the situation doesn't change, will you allow the Lord to change you?
3. What are some practical ways we can all guard against bitterness?

Part 8 *"with joy giving thanks to the Father"*

Chapter 29: These Boots Are Made for Thanking

Discussion Kickoff: What was your absolute worst manners moment? Could you be crowned, "Missed Manners"?

1. If thanks and praise are like keys to the gates of worship, how often do you suppose we try to break in? Do you think we sometimes miss out on sweet times of fellowship in the holy presence of God because we've neglected to thank and praise him?
2. What are some attributes of God that are worthy of praise? What are some blessings he's given that we can thank him for?

3. Are you ready to see your worship climb to new heights? Will you spend time thanking and praising him today?

Chapter 30: Steppin' Out When Your Dogs Are Barking

Discussion Kickoff: What's the 411 on your funniest shoe 911? Are there any wild shoe emergencies you can share?

1. Is there anyone you've seen display unexplainable joy even while experiencing huge trials?
2. Do you tend to live more often "under the circumstances" or "over the circumstances" in those higher places? How does a person get from "under" to "over"? When you need to, are you willing to make that change?
3. Read 1 Peter 1:6–8 again. What are some of the positive results of pain mentioned there? Can you add other positive results that can come from painful experiences?

Chapter 31: The Heels Are Alive

Discussion Kickoff: Do you have an impressive coffee habit? How many cups can you drink in a day and still sleep at night? Could you be in the running for "The Most Likely to Tackle Someone for a Mocha Latte Award"?

1. Thanks-ercising can build the kind of spiritual muscle we need to serve the Lord with zest. Have you been exercising your thanks muscles a little more since you started this section? If so, has that made a difference in your worthy walk? Why do you think offering renewed thanks can change our lives?
2. Can you find inspiration to give thanks and praise in James 1:16–17?

3. Is there room for more thanks and praise in your life? What are some concrete things you can do to grow in this area of the worthy walk?

Chapter 32: Light on Your Feet

Discussion Kickoff: Do you think you might have the most baggage of anyone in the group? Tell about the time you hauled the most, biggest, or strangest luggage.

1. How does remembering that our Father pays attention to our lives and remembering that Jesus is coming again affect how we walk in this life?
2. Whether or not you had an earthly father who handled the role of father well, are you always willing to let God be the perfect Father to you? How does a person's answer to this question affect her life journey?
3. Do you believe the Holy Spirit can speak to a person's heart, convincing that person that God is her loving Heavenly Father? Read through Romans 8:14–16 in the New Living Testament. If you've yet to be convinced, would you be willing to ask him to show you the genuineness of his fatherly love today?

Part 9 *"who has enabled you to share in the saints' inheritance in the light"*

Chapter 33: Walk a Mile in My Pumps

Discussion Kickoff: Do you have an embarrassing pair of comfort-only shoes? Would you be willing to bring them and enter them in the "Oh My Goodness What an Ugly Pair of Shoes" contest?

1. What does it mean that God has "enabled you to share in the saints' inheritance in the light"? Who are the saints?
2. Name some of the amazing things you inherit when you become a child of God. Go ahead, have a little praise fest!
3. According to 1 Peter 1:3–5, how safe is that inheritance? How does that affect how you view your life here on earth?

Chapter 34: Stepping in Time

Discussion Kickoff: What's the most creative application you can come up with for rocket shoes? How about time-travel shoes?

1. Galatians 4:3–5 reminds us that we were once slaves and now we're free. What is the slave life? Have you ever experienced spiritual slavery?
2. What is the free life? What are we free from?
3. Thinking about the love of God and the salvation he provided can certainly change our attitude. How? And how does it change the way we walk?

Chapter 35: Take a Walk on the Light Side

Discussion Kickoff: Is there an embarrassing side to your closet? Anything in there you're trying to keep under your hat? Do you think you might win the "Coming Out of the Closet Award"?

1. According to Ephesians 5:8–14, how should children of light live? Can you think of people you know whose lives shine?
2. In the "Strolling in the Light" section, we're reminded how to avoid darkness. What is that darkness and how do we stay away from it?

3. Look at Luke 11:36. What does the radiant life look like? How do you think your life rates right now on the glow-meter?

Chapter 36: Pedi-cured

Discussion Kickoff: What a trip! What has been your favorite moment through the kickoff section of the *High Heels* journey? Which "Discussion Kickoff" story or contest entry gave you the most ultimate laugh-charge?

1. When did the "life remodel" moment happen to you—when did you make a conscious decision to surrender your life to Jesus as you asked him to come into your life and take control? If you've yet to give your life to him, would you consider praying the suggested prayer in the "You Can Bet Your Life!" section?
2. How does knowing Jesus and seeking to walk worthy affect our happiness? How does it affect our lives?
3. How has the Lord used this book and this discussion time to impact your life? Will you determine to not let the last page of the book or the last meeting of your discussion group be the end of your journey to higher places with the Father? What can you do to keep heading higher still?

Rhonda Rhea is a humor columist and has written hundreds of articles for *HomeLife*, *Today's Christian Woman*, *Marriage Partnership*, *ParentLife*, and dozens more. Also a radio personality, she is a frequent guest of Focus on the Family's *Weekend Magazine* and *Audio Journal*. She is the author of several books, including *I'm Dreaming of Some White Chocolate* and *Who Put the Cat in the Fridge?* Rhonda and her husband, Richie, live in Troy, Missouri, with their five children. She invites you to visit her website at www.rhondarhea.org.

More Bible Studies from ᖇ Revell

for individual or group use

LIFEOVERS

Gain a greater understanding of the God who is in control, even when it doesn't feel like it.

NAKED FRUIT

Explore what it means to be like Christ, and discover how to display the fruit of the Spirit in a way that's uniquely you. A MOPS book.

BREATHE

Gentle, practical advice on how to make time for what matters most. Includes "breathing" exercises. A MOPS book.

OXYGEN

A devotional that helps you take a deep breath for your soul, incorporating spiritual disciplines into your everyday life. A MOPS book.